OUTLAWS & LAWMEN of Western Canada

Volume Two

B.C. policeman Jack Kirkup in 1884. A powerful man who weighed 300 pounds, he believed in "pounding, rather than impounding" cheats, thugs and others who preyed on honest citizens. (See page 4.)

THE COVERS

FRONT: "When Law Dulls the Edge of Chance" by Charles M. Russell, courtesy Buffalo Bill Historical Center, Cody, Wyoming. Russell, 1864-1926, was one of North America's great artists of the Old West and used Southern Alberta and the Mounties as a theme for many paintings.

INSIDE FRONT: Left — North-West Mounted Police Sergeant in the Force's first uniform, 1874. At right is a Sergeant in 1898 dress uniform. Paintings by Tom McNeely, courtesy Rolph-McNally Limited, © Copyright 1973.

PHOTO CREDITS

B.C. Provincial Archives, 4-5, 7, 10, 11, 15, 16, 18, 20, 22, 23, 38-39, 42, 48-49, 56, 86, 87, 93, 96; Glenbow Archives, 12, 58-59, 68, 69, 74, 99, 117; Heritage House, 125; Hudson's Bay Company, 32; Manitoba Archives, 26-27, 52, 53, 55; Provincial Archives of Alberta, 98-99; Public Archives of Canada, 19, 74, 89, 112; Royal Canadian Mounted Police, back cover, 1, 59, 66-67, 71, 76-77, 120-121; Saskatchewan Archives Board, 34-35, 104-105; Tourism B.C., 16, 89; Wells Fargo Bank History Department, 7.

CANADIAN CATALOGUING IN PUBLICATION DATA

Main entry under title: *Outlaws and Lawmen of Western Canada*

ISBN 0-919214-52-5 (v.1). — ISBN 0-919214-54-1 (v. 2)

1. Outlaws — Canada, Western — Biography — Addresses, essays, lectures.*
2. Police — Canada, Western — Biography — Addresses, essays, lectures.*
3. Canada, Western — History — Addresses, essays, lectures.*
FC3217.1.A1 O97   364.1'5'0922   C83-091306-8
F1060.3.O97

Heritage House Publishing Co. Ltd.
#8 - 17921 55 Avenue
Surrey BC V3S 2B3

Printed in Canada

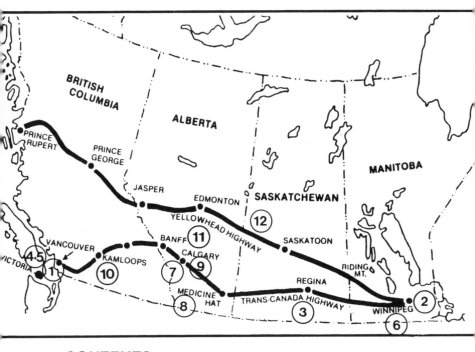

CONTENTS

Western Canada's Pioneer Lawmen

In 1858 when some 30,000 miners armed with rifles, revolvers and bowie knives stampeded to what is today British Columbia, there were only about a dozen unarmed policemen to maintain law and order.

The *S.S. Beaver,* at Victoria in 1862, was the first steam-powered vessel on the entire Pacific Coast. In 1852 she became a court-room for the first jury ever assembled in what became Western Canada. Two Indians were sentenced to death and hanged next morning.

One aspect of British Columbia's history is the refreshing lack of gun-fighters in the province's otherwise colorful past. There is no Billy the Kid, Wyatt Earp, or Wild Bill Hickock, although there should have been. At the province's birth in 1858 all the ingredients were present.

That spring word reached San Francisco that gold had been found to the north on a river that few — if any — locals had heard of. The river was the Fraser, known mainly to the Indians and fur traders of the Hudson's Bay Company. For their part, Company officials were not only satisfied that the region was unknown but deliberately discouraged settlement knowing that farming and fur trading were a poor mixture. Unfortunately for the pioneer firm, on a Sunday morning in April the paddlewheel steamer *Commodore* appeared off Fort Victoria at the southern tip of Vancouver Island. Some 500 hopeful goldseekers disembarked, followed in the next few months by over 30,000 more. The quiet, fur trading post

was suddenly a jamboree of tents. Land that previously couldn't find a buyer at $5 an acre was soon $3,000 an acre. Stores, hotels and saloons appeared — particularly the saloons — the perfect setting for growth of the gunfighters.

Furthermore, there was no shortage of rifles or revolvers. "He was a gaunt, stringy, dried-up looking Kentuckian, with a gutta-percha face, sunk into which . . . twinkled two all alive and piercing eyes . . . ." wrote author Kinahan Cornwallis of one miner. "He carried a couple of revolvers, and a bowie knife, with the point of which he took the opportunity of picking his teeth immediately after supper."

Another writer in June 1858 noted of the Americans: "They were all . . . equipped with the universal revolver, many of them carrying a brace of such, as well as a bowie knife."

In addition to the incoming miners — most of whom were law abiding — there were others who were not. They were the outlaws, many of them chased from American mining camps by vigilante committees. But when these renegades arrived at the tent-town of Fort Victoria, ready to acquire gold by means other than mining, they received a shock. A month after the first swarm of miners stepped ashore a local ordinance banned the belt gun. That was that. Potential Billy the Kids and Wild Bill Hickocks never had a chance to flourish.

One thug whose potential crime career was blunted in Victoria was Boone Helm — and he was a thug. Gunfighter, murderer, thief, he had robbed stages, bribed judges and juries, and cold-bloodedly killed a partner whose only offence was that he had agreed to go to California with Helm then changed his mind. Helm was also a cannibal. Once on a trip to Walla Walla (in today's Washington) to Salt Lake City with a race horse, roulette wheel and 200 decks of cards, he subsisted for a week on the leg of a dead companion. He even carried it across his shoulder between meals so that it would be handy. When he met an Indian on the trail it was too much for the Indian and he threw up.

Anyhow, Helm thought he would check out the new gold rush. As part of his surveillance he stepped into the Adelphi Saloon at Yates and Government Streets in the rapidly building Victoria and ordered a drink. Then he refused to pay for it. He probably felt that the sound of his name was good for a drink anywhere. In fact he said so.

The bartender, however, wasn't impressed. He called a policeman and Boone was escorted to the local lockup. This development was indeed embarrassing since in a thirteen-year career as an outlaw he had never been jailed. Worse, he was fined $25. But now his pride took over and he refused to pay it. The alternative was a couple of weeks washing floors, windows and anything else that needed cleaning. Then the bold bandit was shipped back to the U.S. But he obviously had learned little.

In 1864 Helm and four of his pals were rounded up by a vigilante committee in Virginia City, Montana. But unlike Victoria's lawmen they didn't bother with the formalities of a courtroom. They simply hanged the lot. Ironically, by dying, Helm became better known than when he lived. The building in which he and his four companions kicked their lives away still stands, rope burns visible on the rafters. It and the five graves

Like the above men in California, Boone Helm was hanged by a vigilante committee, a common occurrence in the U.S. during the frontier era. By contrast, men such as Governor Douglas, inset, firmly established law and order in the region that became the province of British Columbia.

are popular tourist attractions in Virginia City.

By 1864 when Helm stood on a box which was then booted from under him, massive changes had occurred in the former Hudson's Bay Company fur preserve. Although sand and gravel bars on the Fraser River had in 1858-59 yielded millions in gold, the ever restless miners surged upstream. Some 640 km (400 miles) to the north at the headwaters of one of the river's major tributaries they uncovered the mother lode. The region became known as the Cariboo and by 1865 was to yield some $50 million — with gold selling at $16 an ounce.

Despite this treasure which attracted men good and bad from around the world, the region was remarkably law abiding. In 1862 a correspondent for the *Times* newspaper in London wrote: "As to security of life, I consider it just as safe here as in England."

The reason dated back to 1849 when Vancouver Island was proclaimed a Crown Colony and the existing laws of England applied. A judge was appointed, but with a population of under 100 there was no crime. If there were some recalcitrant Indians up the coast, the Governor, James Douglas, sent a gunboat to shell them and that was that. An exception was in 1852 when the Hudson's Bay Company *Beaver,* first steam vessel on the Pacific Coast, was used as a court room for the first jury ever assembled in the West. Two Indians were found guilty of murdering a shepherd and hanged the next morning.

With the gold rush of 1858 Governor Douglas appointed Augustus C. Pemberton as Commissioner of Police — the first in the 3,000-km- (2,000-miles-) long region that became Western Canada. Under him was Superintendent Horace Smith and about a dozen constables. Although all were unarmed they quickly established themselves as peacekeepers.

Take one gang called the Forty Thieves which had terrorized San Francisco. Lured by the new gold strike, several ventured north. All were rounded up within a week and shipped back. Perhaps the presence of Constable Joe Eden hastened their peaceful exit. He was a prize-fighter and in those days it was straight bare knuckles with a fight lasting until the opponent was unconscious or surrendered. One of Joe's triumphs over a challenger named George Baker lasted nearly two hours and went for 128 rounds. Joe won $500 and next day was back on duty.

The police force formed by Governor Douglas and A. Pemberton, however, had jurisdiction only on Vancouver Island. The task of organizing the second group of lawmakers in Western Canada fell to an Irishman, Chartres Brew. In 1858 he was appointed by Sir Edward Bulwer Lytton, Britain's Secretary of State for the Colonies, to organize a force to keep order in the new gold colony. Brew had already served with distinction in the Crimean War and had fourteen years experience in the Royal Irish Constabulary. An item in *The Victoria Gazette* in November 1858 noted: "The steamer *Beaver* . . . sailed for Fort Langley yesterday morning. She had on board Captain Grant and his company of Royal Engineers, and Captain Brew, the new commissioner of police for British Columbia. It is the intention of Captain Brew to organize an efficient force in the new colony immediately . . . ."

The first problem Brew encountered was finding men for his force.

". . . it will be extremely difficult to find men in British Columbia fit for the police," he wrote. "The class of men who now offer themselves for enrollment are, with few exceptions, persons not to be trusted as peace officers.

"They are chiefly miners who would never become obedient subordinates or submit themselves to the strict discipline which must always be maintained in an armed corps.

"These men, besides, merely want employment for the winter months and are determined to return to their mining pursuits on the opening of spring, so that just when they know something of their duties and their services were most needed they would abandon the force."

He asked Governor Douglas to send for members of the Royal Irish Constabulary, in the meanwhile enrolling men he felt would fulfill the awesome responsibility. How well he succeeded was summarized by northwest historian H.H. Bancroft when he wrote: "Never in the pacification and settlement of any section of America have there been so few disturbances, so few crimes against law and order."

Not only were the policemen thinly spread — one to nearly 10,360 sq. km (4,000 sq. miles) — they had to cope with a land which extended some 640 km (400 miles) from the Pacific Ocean to the Rocky Mountains, and for another 1,600 km (1,000 miles) south to north. There are many recorded instances of when they brought their prisoners by horseback, stagecoach and canoe 640 km (400 miles) and more to a courtroom. They were to police British Columbia for nearly a century until the RCMP took over provincial law enforcement duties.

In the pioneer days of the force the constables evolved their own way of dealing with rowdies. Since they didn't have to contend with lawyers who consider it their duty to defend punks and hoods — at public expense, of course — the policemen could be original in their method of peace-keeping. Take Jack Kirkup who stood 190 cm (6 ft. 3 ins.) and weighed 136 kg (300 lbs.)

Of him, B.C. historian Elsie G. Turnbull wrote: "Constable Kirkup treated the unruly element with a heavy hand. His method of control consisted of 'pounding instead of impounding offenders.' A typical instance concerned the visit of a hairy-chested tough from Kaslo to Revelstoke in the Arrow-Kootenay Lakes region of B.C. This man was in the habit of shaking dice in a saloon and if he won would shake again. If he lost he would refuse to pay. He would laugh, stroll away and call out: 'That's the way we do things in Kaslo!'

"One saloon-keeper, in anger, hit him with a two-by-four and a crowd gathered. Kirkup waited until the man regained consciousness, but instead of arresting him took him to the edge of town. Here he started the dice-shaker off toward Kaslo with the words: 'Tell 'em in Kaslo that's the way we do things in Revelstoke.' "

In his "pounding instead of impounding" policy, Kirkup was aided by a walking cane presented by an ex-convict. Made of leather and silver trimmed, it not only looked pretty but was functional too, since it had an embedded steel rod and weighted butt. As Elsie Turnbull observed: "Wielded by the powerful constable it became a lethal weapon that effectively quietened any potential disturber of the peace.''

Kirkup's answer to drunkenness was to lock up the drunk then go after the saloon keeper. "Many a bartender learned to keep his difficult customers out of sight until they were normal again," Elsie Turnbull noted. "Kirkup sometimes encouraged 'tanked' miners to fight, believing a little exercise would help work the whiskey out of their pores. If men were long on talk and short on performance it wasn't unknown for Kirkup to bump heads together until he got them mad and then set them down to finish it.''

Then there is the story of a boxing match in Rossland staged by two shysters from Spokane. Unfortunately for them, Kirkup was chosen to referee. Knowing that they had been faking their bouts, he brought them together in the ring. "Boys," he said quietly, "I don't want to see any flim flam here. I want to see a spirited exhibition. And to ensure that it is, the loser's going to get three months in jail.''

While Kirkup's peacekeeping methods were perhaps unorthodox, they achieved their objective. But in achieving this objective the thinly spread policemen had formidable allies, especially during the force's formative years. These allies were judges such as John Carmichael Haynes, Peter O'Reilly and Matthew Baillie Begbie. They rode enormous distances while performing their duties, holding court in log cabins, tents and even astride their saddle horse.

John Carmichael Haynes was twenty-seven when he landed in British Columbia on Christmas Day in 1858 to join Brew's police force. In 1860

In 1858 A. Pemberton, above, became Commissioner of Police for the Crown Colony of Vancouver Island. He had about a dozen men to control some 30,000 gold-hungry miners. Chartres Brew, above right, had about the same number of men to police the neighboring Crown Colony of British Columbia — a region fifty per cent larger than France. The photo on the opposite page shows Victoria in the early 1860s.

he was appointed Deputy Collector of Customs in the Okanagan-Similkameen region of southern British Columbia, and in 1864 to Justice of the Peace. Like other frontier justices, he travelled on horseback, identified by his Irish frieze jacket, well cut riding breeches, and polished English riding boots. In summer he wore a pith helmet, in winter a more practical felt hat, but never a Stetson which he considered undignified. Quiet, well informed and gentlemanly, wherever he went he was the law.

Shortly after his appointment in 1864, Haynes with Constable Young set out from the Okanagan for the new mining community of Wild Horse Creek in the shadow of the Rocky Mountains some 480 km (300 miles) to the east. After twenty days in the saddle they reached Wild Horse, a community of some fifty cabins, a few dance halls and gambling joints and a brewery. The day before Haynes arrived it had also been the scene of a blazing gunfight which left one man dead and one badly wounded.

Gold had been discovered at Wild Horse Creek the year before and in the area were upwards of 2,000 miners — most of them heavily armed. The only law was of the home-made variety, a type of vigilante committee under Robert Dore. The problem was that there were two factions in the camp. The majority were U.S. citizens, led by a trio named "Yeast Powder" Bill Burmister, "Overland" Bob Evans and Neil Dougherty. The Canadian minority was headed by a fiery and vocal young Irishman, Thomas Walker. The two groups met on the hot afternoon of August 9 in front of the Fortier Cafe.

An argument erupted and Walker pulled his revolver. He fired point

Wild Horse Creek in 1883 when the gold was exhausted and most of the miners had left. Thomas Walker's grave has been preserved over the years by public-spirited citizens of the Wild Horse region.

blank at Yeast Powder Bill but, unfortunately for Walker, he only shot the end off Yeast Powder's thumb. Before Walker could fire again the American drew one of his two guns with his undamaged hand. He pulled the trigger and Walker dropped, a bullet in his heart.

Overland Bob Evans then started shooting and a free-for-all ensued. When the fracas ended casualties included Overland Bob so badly wounded that he was three months recovering, a man named Kelly stabbed in the back, and another called Paddy Skie clubbed so hard that he was unconscious for months.

An account of subsequent events was written by D.M. Drumheller in his book, *"Uncle Dan" Drumheller Tells Thrills of Western Trails* . . . . . "A mob was quickly raised by the friends of Tommy Walker for the purpose of hanging Overland Bob and Yeast Powder Bill. Then a law and order organization numbering about 1,000 miners, of which I was a member, assembled. It was the purpose of our organization to order a miners' court and give all concerned a fair trial. Our organization took care of the . . . wounded men and put a strong guard around them. The next morning we appointed a lawyer by the name of A.J. Gregory as trial judge and John McClellan sheriff, with authority to appoint as many deputies as he wished. That was the condition of things when Judge Haines (Haynes), the British Columbia Commissioner, rode into camp.

" 'Fifteen hundred men under arms in the queen's dominion. A dastardly usurpation of authority, don't cher know,' remarked Judge Haines. But one little English constable with knee breeches, red cap, cane in his hand, riding a jockey saddle and mounted on a bob-tailed horse, quelled that mob in 15 minutes."

Haynes relieved the "sheriff" of further duties and held an inquest. Although the jury was confused about who shot whom in the gun duel, they felt that Yeast Powder Bill had acted in self defence. A subsequent preliminary hearing agreed and Yeast Powder Bill was set free.

To prevent a reoccurrence, Haynes decreed that revolvers were to be kept at home. The consequence was impressive. A short time later when Colonial Secretary Arthur N. Birch reached Wild Horse after twenty-four days on horseback from the Fraser River, he reported: "I found the British Columbia mining laws in full force, all customs duties paid, no pistols to be seen and everything as quiet and orderly as it could possibly be in the most civilized district of the colony."

But it was inevitable that a price would be paid by those responsible for maintaining everything "quiet and orderly." Near the community of Bella Coola on the B.C. Coast on May 6, 1865, the 80-ton trading schooner *Langley* swung at anchor in a little bay. Forward in the ship's fo'c'sle an oil lamp swinging in a gimbal cast eerie shadows as skipper Smith poked some wood in the stove preparatory to making coffee. Nearby, on a locker, sat big, bearded B.C. Police Constable J.D.B. "Jack" Ogilvie, sole representative of the law between Cape Caution and the Skeena River — 320 km (200 miles) as the crow flies but several thousand along the fjords which characterize the region.

As the men talked, they didn't notice the door of the forward chain locker slowly open. From it peered a crafty, evil-looking face, thin, unshaven with eyes deep set and treacherous. The man behind the face — thirty-five-year-old French-Canadian Antoine Lucanage — raised a heavy Colt revolver, levelled it at the unsuspecting police officer and pulled the trigger.

The crashing report rocked the little cabin. In an acrid, billowing cloud of black-powder smoke Ogilvie got slowly to his feet then slumped down. Skipper Smith, with one quick glance at the gunman's hideout, fled up the companionway to the deck. There he found Morris Moss, a coastal fur trader and Ogilvie's friend.

A few days earlier Ogilvie had asked Moss to help him capture some renegade whites who were selling liquor to the Indians. Chief of them was Antoine Lucanage who on April 1, 1865, in broad daylight boldly sailed right into Bella Coola. He and his boat were seized by Ogilvie and Lucanage was shipped to jail at New Westminster on a passing schooner.

On the way he jumped overboard at the south end of Johnstone Strait and despite swirling tide rips miraculously reached shore. He was later picked up by the *Langley* whose skipper was unaware that Lucanage was on his way to jail. By a strange quirk of fate Bella Coola was among her stopping places. At Bella Coola Lucanage slipped ashore at night. When Ogilvie heard of the incident he mustered some Indians and searched the area but found no trace of the fugitive.

A couple of days later when the *Langley* left, Ogilvie had a hunch that Lucanage had somehow regained the vessel. "Let's catch her up and search her," was his quick suggestion to Moss.

With six swiftly paddling Indians the pair set off and about four hours later caught the schooner. Her skipper Smith swore that the fugitive wasn't aboard. Ten minutes later came the dramatic moment when Lucanage fired the shot from the chain locker.

Smith rushed up on deck to incoherently tell his story to Moss, who promptly grabbed a lantern to go down in the fo'c'sle after the gunman. At that moment, however, Ogilvie staggered up on deck. Then Lucanage appeared, knife in one hand, revolver in the other.

Constable Ogilvie, though mortally wounded, grappled with the cutthroat and wrested the gun from him. Then, as Lucanage turned and ran towards a companionway, Ogilvie fired two shots at him. Moss, aft at the wheel, drew his revolver and ran forward but the mainsail boom swung over and hurled him into the water. The Indians in the canoe heard him yell and picked him up.

When Moss got back on board he noticed that Ogilvie was near total collapse. He and Smith packed the wounded man below, and as they were doing so Lucanage escaped in a skiff. Below deck, Ogilvie lived only a few more minutes.

The murder stirred the Colony and the government offered a $1,000 reward for Lucanage's capture. Despite the reward and a protracted search he was never found alive, although he was variously reported as far south as San Francisco. Finally, several months later a corpse was found on northern Vancouver Island and identified as Lucanage. One story is that he had escaped with the aid of Indian canoemen and promised them blankets in return. Once on Vancouver Island he had tried to escape

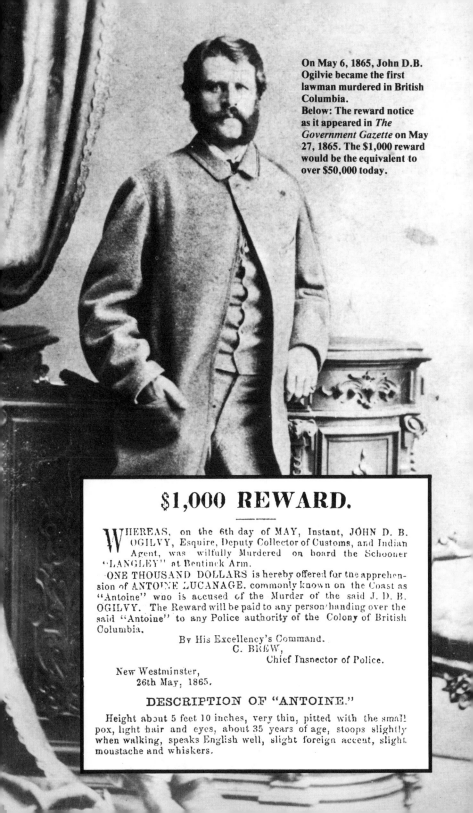

On May 6, 1865, John D.B. Ogilvie became the first lawman murdered in British Columbia.
Below: The reward notice as it appeared in *The Government Gazette* on May 27, 1865. The $1,000 reward would be the equivalent to over $50,000 today.

$1,000 REWARD.

WHEREAS, on the 6th day of MAY, Instant, JOHN D. B. OGILVY, Esquire, Deputy Collector of Customs, and Indian Agent, was wilfully Murdered on board the Schooner "LANGLEY" at Bentinck Arm.

ONE THOUSAND DOLLARS is hereby offered for the apprehension of ANTOINE LUCANAGE, commonly known on the Coast as "Antoine" who is accused of the Murder of the said J. D. B. OGILVY. The Reward will be paid to any person handing over the said "Antoine" to any Police authority of the Colony of British Columbia.

By His Excellency's Command.
C. BREW,
Chief Inspector of Police.

New Westminster,
26th May, 1865.

DESCRIPTION OF "ANTOINE."

Height about 5 feet 10 inches, very thin, pitted with the small pox, light hair and eyes, about 35 years of age, stoops slightly when walking, speaks English well, slight foreign accent, slight moustache and whiskers.

Pioneer Judges Peter O'Reilly, left, and J.C. Haynes, with Osoyoos Lake in the Southern Okanagan where Haynes in 1860 began his career as a lawman.

without paying his debt and the Indians killed him. Had they known of the reward, they could have been $1,000 richer.

A similar type of justice avenged the second policeman to die on duty. After Judge J.C. Haynes in 1864 journeyed to Wild Horse Creek to bring law and order, three constables were subsequently stationed there. They were James Carrington, Jimmy Normansell and Jack Lawson, a young man from New Brunswick.

In 1867 while Normansell and Carrington were on patrol, two Dutch ranchers rode into Wild Horse and reported that their horses had been stolen and that they had tracked the thief to a camp about 6.5 km (4 miles) away. Lawson accompanied the two back to the camp and after about an hour spotted the thief coming down the trail.

The constable stopped him, and as he asked about the horses noticed the man's hand slipping inside his jacket. Lawson promptly drew his gun and gave curt instructions to get his hands in the air. Lawson then turned to call one of the ranchers forward — a split second error which cost him his life. With a lightning draw, the thief put a bullet through the back of the policeman's head. As the hapless constable reeled in the saddle and slipped to the ground, it was the cue for the Dutchmen to spur their horses. The thief coolly took the constable's gun then left in the opposite direction.

The man who had murdered Lawson was Charlie "One Ear" Brown, well known to Victoria police. His first conviction in the community was November 3, 1859, for peddling whiskey. After a spell at hard labor, which consisted of tamping rocks to hard-surface the young community's streets while wearing leg irons, he was freed. But not for long. He was soon back on the chain gang for swindling an Indian. In 1861 he was back twice, the second time he received a one-year sentence and a nickname, "One Ear," that would later considerably help the cause of justice.

The nickname was born one afternoon when jailer Charles B. Wright got orders to move Brown to another cell. When Wright entered the cell, Brown backed against the wall and muttered: "You lay a hand on me you son of a bitch and I'll murder you."

In the ensuing struggle Brown got a head lock on the jailer, but Wright managed to draw his gun. Working the muzzle close to Brown's ear he gave a crisp order. "Let go, or I'll blow your head off."

In reply, Brown increased the pressure. In response, Wright squeezed the trigger. Brown was fortunate that he lost only his ear. In return he gained a nickname and another year on the street gang for assaulting a peace officer. He soon tired of tamping rocks, however, and feigned illness to get into hospital. Two days later he escaped, believed to be headed for the Cariboo. Instead he did a little horse stealing in the Fraser Valley then heard about the riches at Wild Horse Creek. He headed eastward via the United States, continuing his horse stealing as the two Dutch ranchers knew from first hand experience.

After One Ear Brown shot Lawson and headed for the border, the ranchers galloped back to Wild Horse. In the absence of the policemen they told their story to a silent and grim-eyed group of miners. Four of the listeners exchanged glances and broke away from the group. They saddled up, made sure their shotguns were loaded and left to avenge the murder.

They discovered that One Ear had crossed the St. Mary's River on a raft and had lost most of his supplies in the rough water. Next they reined their sweating horses at Joe Davis' camp where they learned that the lop-eared bandit had got some grub. Some distance further on the four vigilantes came on a lone Chinese. Yes, he had seen a man. Yes, he had a missing ear. He wanted ammunition but the man didn't have any.

On they pressed, next checking with a blacksmith who said the earless fugitive had got some grub from him. He was still armed, and boastfully recounted how he'd killed a B.C. policeman and was going to shoot a couple of Dutchmen as soon as he got the chance. Not long afterward the self-appointed lawmen reached the Idaho border but dispensed with the formalities of a legal crossing. As they neared Bonner's Ferry they met an Indian who told them that he had been accosted by a horseman — a man minus one ear, a man who wanted ammunition. It was then the four miners realized that they had outrun their quarry and if they circled back could cut him off.

The result was reported later in the *British Columbian* newspaper at New Westminster: "Leaving their jaded horses at the ferry, and disguising themselves with moccasins, etc., they pushed forward . . . and lay in wait for him. Seeing no footprints of either man or beast on the trail, Brown pressed on, thinking himself safe. They soon saw him advancing at a rapid pace, with a remaining pistol in one hand and a knife in the other. Three of them raised their guns, double-barrelled guns, loaded with buckshot,

The jail in Victoria where Charlie Brown earned his nickname "One Ear." Between 1860 and 1885 nine men were hanged in the jail yard.
Rock Creek, opposite page in 1861, was typical of scores of mining communities like Wild Horse which flourished briefly then waned as the gold was removed.

and fired simultaneously, literally riddling his dastardly carcass. Returning the following day, they dug a hole into which they put the remains of Charles Brown, the thief and cowardly murderer. He lies close by the side of Walla Walla trail, 43 miles south of the boundary line.''

Since the episode happened across the border, B.C.'s reputation of never having had a murderer disposed of by vigilantes remained unsullied.

While events leading to the tragic murder of Constable Lawson were unfurling, Judge J.C. Haynes' duties at Wild Horse had been assumed by another Irishman, Peter O'Reilly. He came to British Columbia in 1858 and in April 1859 was appointed assistant gold commissioner, then stipendiary magistrate. In forthcoming years he served in many regions where gold was discovered, including the Cariboo, Omineca, Big Bend and Wild Horse Creek. At Wild Horse he gave an address which has become a British Columbia legend.

Since there was no stenographer to record his words there are many versions of what he said. Possibly the most accurate is in a book called *Sport and Life in the Hunting Grounds of Western America and British Columbia*. It was written by W.A. Baillie-Grohman, a sportsman-developer who arrived in the East Kootenay in 1882. According to Baillie-Grohman, when O'Reilly arrived at Wild Horse he addressed a group of miners in front of "the single-roomed cabin which he had turned into a temporary courthouse . . . and made a famous speech which is still remembered throughout the mining camps . . . . Standing near the pole from which floated the Union Jack . . . he said: 'Boys, I am here to keep

A problem for British Columbia lawmen was the mountainous nature of the province. As a consequence, for decades roads were few and prisoners transported hundreds of miles by canoes, saddle horses, stagecoaches and sternwheel steamers.

The sternwheeler is at Yale on the Fraser River in the 1880s; the stagecoach at Ashcroft in 1890. Stagecoaches served the Central Interior for fifty years.

order and to administer the law. Those who don't want law and order can "git," but those who stay with the camp, remember on what side of the line the camp is; for, boys, if there is shooting in Kootenay there will be hanging in Kootenay.' "

The only problem with the address is that some authors attribute it to Judge Haynes. In his book, however, Baillie-Grohman notes: "Two old miners, Clark and Doyle, who were present on the occasion, gave me this version of Judge O'Reilly's speech. It varies but triflingly from Bancroft's version. (Bancroft was a famous Pacific Northwest historian.) When I asked Mr. O'Reilly for the real version, he told me he had long forgotten the exact words he had used."

Support for O'Reilly being the originator — and also an indication of the respect accorded him by the miners — is contained in another book, *Ocean to Ocean*. It is an account of an 1872 expedition across Canada led by Sandford Fleming, the Canadian Pacific Railway's engineer-in-chief. On October 1, 1872, at Ashcroft Manor the expedition's secretary, Reverend G.M. Grant, wrote: "This evening we met Judge O'Reilly whose praises had been often sung by Brown and Beaupre (packers and ex-miners hired near Fort Edmonton to care for the expedition's packhorses). 'There isn't the gold in British Columbia that would bribe Judge O'Reilly,' was their emphatic endorsement of his dealings with the miners. They described him, arriving as the representative of British law and order, at Kootenie, (one of many variations in the spelling of "Kootenay") immediately after thousands had flocked to the newly discovered gold mines there. Assembling them, he said that order must and would be kept; and advised them not to display their revolvers unnecessarily, 'for, boys, if there's shooting in Kootenie, there will be hanging . . . .' "

Three days after meeting Judge O'Reilly, Fleming's expedition boarded the sternwheel steamer *Onward* at Yale and met another judge, Matthew Baillie Begbie, the most famous of all British Columbia's lawmen. Reverend Grant wrote: "On board the 'Onward' we met Chief Justice Begbie, another man held in profound respect by the miners, Siwashes, and all others among whom he has dealt out justice. Judge Lynch has never been required in British Columbia, because Chief Justice Begbie did his duty . . . . It is a grand sight to see . . . a British judge backed by one or two constables maintaining order at the gold mines among the . . . gamblers, claim 'jumpers' and cutthroats who congregate at such places . . . ."

Like Police Inspector Chartres Brew, Begbie had been selected in 1858 by Sir Edward Bulwer Lytton to help maintain order in British Columbia. Since the new judge had to spend weeks in the saddle because there were no roads in the hundreds of miles of wilderness, Lytton wanted a young, athletic man. He also, in Lytton's own words: "Must be a man who could, if necessary, truss a murderer up and hang him from the nearest tree."

Begbie arrived in British Columbia on November 16, 1858, and three days later was appointed judge, the only one in a region that covered an area larger than most of Europe. It was a dramatic change for a man who a few months before was a struggling barrister in England. While he personally never had to "truss a murderer up and hang him from the nearest tree," he quickly established a record for fearlessness and impartial justice.

For instance during the gold rush in a saloon at Williams Lake in the Cariboo a U.S. citizen named Gilchrist attempted to shoot a man named Turner. But as Gilchrist pulled the trigger someone bumped him and the bullet killed a man leaning on the bar, fast asleep.

As Dr. W.W. Walkem noted in his book, *Stories of Early British Columbia:* "The case subsequently came before Judge Begbie, and a jury chosen from a class of people composed of many fugitives from justice from the American side, and known to be horse thieves from The Dalles, Oregon. (In the early days of the gold rush there were seldom enough British subjects for a jury and U.S. residents were sworn in — without too many questions asked.)

"After a very patient hearing of the evidence, which was clear and uncontradicted, Judge Begbie charged the jury very strongly against the

The Cariboo mining community of Richfield in 1868, at lower left the modest log courthouse with its flagpole of authority.
At right is Judge Matthew Baillie Begbie who earned a reputation as ". . . the damndest man that ever came over the Cariboo road."

prisoner, at the same time severely condemning the carrying of weapons of a dangerous and deadly character. He warned the jury against being carried away by sympathy, or by the accidental nature of the shooting. The prisoner in attempting to kill one man had killed another. That was murder . . . .

"The jury retired, and after an absence of thirty minutes returned with a verdict of 'manslaughter.' Turning to the prisoner, the chief justice said: '. . . It is far from a pleasant duty for me to have to sentence you only to imprisonment for life. I feel I am, through some incomprehensible reason, prevented from doing my proper duty . . . . Your crime was unmitigated, diabolical murder. You deserve to be hanged! Had the jury performed their duty I might now have the painful satisfaction of condemning you to death, and you, gentlemen of the jury, you are a pack of Dalles horse thieves, and permit me to say, it would give me great pleasure to see you hanged, each and every one of you, for declaring a murderer guilty only of manslaughter.''

Another incident involved an Irishman named Davie Lavin charged with murder following a fist fight with Johnston Robertson in Victoria's Regent Saloon. Robertson died three days later of brain injuries. The jury felt that Lavin was not totally responsible since Robertson had been involved in several other fights during the afternoon. They decided that one additional punch wasn't necessarily the cause of death and acquitted him.

Begbie was furious at the verdict. "Gentlemen of the Jury," he said to them, "I have heard your verdict. But mind you; it's your verdict, not mine. On your conscience will rest the stigma of returning such a disgraceful verdict and one at variance with the evidence on which you have sworn to find the guilt or innocence of the prisoner. Many repetitions of such conduct as yours will make trial by jury a horrible farce and the city of Victoria, which you inhabit, a nest of immorality and crime encouraged by immunity from the law which criminals will receive from the announcement of such verdicts as yours. I have nothing more to say to you."

Begbie then turned to Lavin. "Prisoner, you are discharged! Go, and sandbag some of the jurymen! They deserve it!"

But not only errant jurors felt Begbie's wrath; law-breakers quickly learned that the Judge had little sympathy for them. During the spring assizes in 1861 a man named John Burke received nine months hard labor for stealing two pairs of blankets. Two Chinese found guilty of stealing a pistol got two years at hard labor.

In addition to a jail term, he frequently imposed a flogging with the dreaded "cat o' nine tails." Police Inspector Chartres Brew objected to flogging but Begbie defended it in a letter to Governor Douglas: "My idea is that if a man insists of behaving like a brute, after a fair warning, & won't quit the Colony; treat him like a brute & flog him."

(While this statement may give the impression that Begbie was merciless, he really wasn't. He disliked imposing the death penalty but it was the law and he had no choice. Flogging was also the law and remained so in Canada until about 1930. In 1924, for instance, Bill Bagley, leader of a gang which had robbed the Royal Bank in Nanaimo, received ten years in jail and twenty lashes.)

Begbie's stern insistence that everyone obey the law or pay the penalty soon built him a reputation for impartiality and firmness. On one occasion after a shooting escapade miners themselves apprehended those involved and held them, knowing Begbie would arrive as soon as he learned of the incident. He held court wherever convenient: a settler's cabin, a barn, a tent or even while sitting on his horse, always properly dressed in his robes and wig.

The result of Begbie's firmness was noted in the *Victoria Colonist* on August 17, 1863, in a news report on the absence of crime around the Cariboo goldfields: "Everything is very quiet and orderly on (Williams) Creek owing in great measure to Mr. O'Reilly's efficiency and the wholesome presence of Judge Begbie who seems to be a terror to evil doers and a sworn enemy to the use of the knife and revolver. Crime in Cariboo has been vigorously checked in its infancy by a firm hand, and seems to have sought some soil more congenial to its growth . . . ."

Judge Begbie would continue to dispense justice with his "firm hand" for over thirty years after that newspaper item. In 1870 he was saddened by the sudden death of Chartres Brew, the province's first policeman. In 1867 Brew had been transferred to Cariboo as magistrate and gold commissioner with headquarters at Barkerville. But the harsh climate of the mountains and deplorable living conditions while travelling the district affected his health and he died at fifty-five.

On his grave in Barkerville is the following epitaph, written by Judge Begbie: "A man imperturbable in courage and temper, endowed with a great & varied administrative capacity, a most ready wit, a most pure integrity, and a most humane heart."

Begbie also described the harsh conditions endured by Brew and other judicial officials while on circuit, living in a tent and cooking over an open fire: "The climate in Cariboo is at times exceedingly wet, as in all high mountainous regions — and it is not unusual to have torrents of rain for a week . . . almost without intermission. The tent being the same as my own — and although it answers very well in tolerable weather or even for a few days of rain, and where the camp is changed from time to time, I find that my tent becomes occasionally covered with mildew in the inside while it is impossible to keep books etc. dry, and all writing & recording is carried on at the greatest inconvenience. Besides, the ground being constantly cold & damp, and there being no opportunity of approaching a fire without going out into the heavy rain, all cooking, or drying any articles of apparel becomes extremely irksome; and all officers who have to remain for any length of time in that district ought to (be provided) at least with one room having a fireplace where they may at least be sure to meet a dry place to lie on, and the means of warming themselves and drying their clothes, keeping their books etc. and placing a table so to be able to write."

The same year that Brew died Begbie was appointed Chief Justice of the Crown Colony of British Columbia and when B.C. joined confederation in 1871, Chief Justice of the Province of British Columbia. He continued his career for over twenty years after Confederation, becoming Sir Matthew Baillie Begbie and hearing his last case on May 1, 1894, when he was seventy-five. A little over a month later he died. Although the Judge wished for a quiet funeral such was his reputation that the provincial government decreed that he was to have a state funeral. One of the pallbearers was Premier Theodore Davie, and among the mourners, Peter O'Reilly, who had become a close friend. In his excellent biography of Begbie, ". . . *The Man For a New Country,* author David R. Williams notes that "Victoria has not since witnessed a funeral equal to it . . . ."

Of assessments made about the Chief Justice, a miner wrote the most unorthodox when he noted: "Begbie was the biggest man, the smartest man, the best looking man, and the damndest man that ever came over the Cariboo road."

While Begbie probably would have considered the tribute too flattering, he would undoubtedly have agreed that much of it also applied to Police Inspector Chartres Brew and his few constables, to Judge Haynes and Judge O'Reilly, and to all other pioneer lawmen who maintained order in a frontier land.

Manitoba's First Official Outlaw

**Although brawling Gilbert Godon was
not the first man to break the law in what is
today Western Canada, he did become
Manitoba's first official outlaw.**

The distinction of being Manitoba's first official outlaw goes to Gilbert
Godon, a stout, poker-faced young Metis from Red Lake district. He
came into prominence in the troubled times that followed the first Riel
uprising of 1869-70. There was a great deal of ill feeling between the
occupation troops sent from Canada and the half-breeds of Fort Garry

and St. Boniface. Godon, a man of quick movement and decisive action, allied himself with the soldiers and was frequently found swinging his fists or a bottle on their behalf.

A favorite off-duty haunt for the soldiers was Fort Garry's (now Winnipeg) Pride of the West Saloon operated by Dugald Sinclair. It was also frequented by Metis, the native born French-Canadian halfbreeds. Usually the two groups managed to avoid each other — the soldiers by

A group of Metis outside Winnipeg's Red Saloon about 1872.

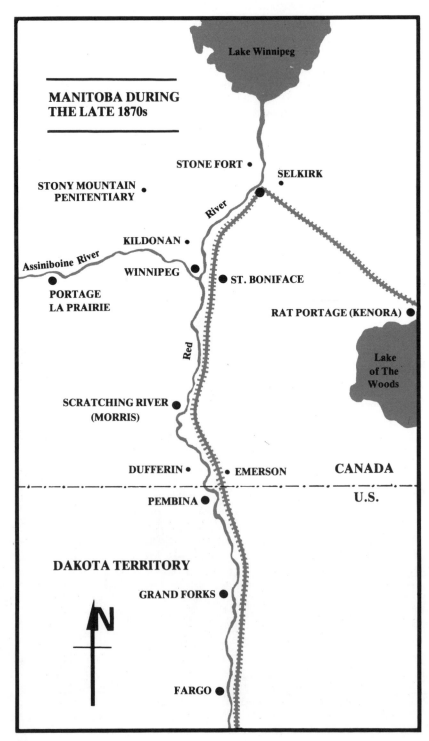

MANITOBA DURING
THE LATE 1870s

Lake Winnipeg

STONE FORT •
• SELKIRK

STONY MOUNTAIN
PENITENTIARY •

River

KILDONAN •

Assiniboine River

WINNIPEG •
• ST. BONIFACE

PORTAGE
LA PRAIRIE •

RAT PORTAGE (KENORA) •

Lake
of The
Woods

Red

SCRATCHING RIVER
(MORRIS) •

DUFFERIN •
• EMERSON   CANADA

U.S.

PEMBINA •

DAKOTA TERRITORY

N

GRAND FORKS •

FARGO •

28

visiting during the day and the Metis in the evening — but occasionally their visits coincided and invariably led to friction.

On one of these occasions during a pitched battle between Metis and soldiers someone pulled a revolver and fired at innkeeper Sinclair who was vainly trying to halt the melee. Gilbert Godon flung himself on the would-be assassin and took the bullet intended for Sinclair in his right arm. A few minutes later, reinforcements arrived from the barracks and the Metis left. Godon's wound was treated by a local doctor and the whole incident written off by the police of the recently-formed province of Manitoba as a demonstration of youthful exuberance.

Drinking and brawling continued to be popular pastimes at Red River during the early 1870s, and Godon was frequently found in the middle of these activities. Nothing unduly serious happened until the night of October 10, 1873, when Godon and a group of drinking pals arrived at the Dufferin home of A.J. Fawcett who sold liquor illegally. Most of the group had already tilted the bottle high at a similar outlet and when Fawcett refused to serve them he was pushed and threatened by Benjamin Marchand who promised violence if the whiskey was not produced quickly.

Godon, with his penchant for defending bartenders, intervened and chased Marchand outside. Marchand's son, Benjamin, retaliated by seizing a shovel and banging it lustily on Godon's head. A wild slug-fest erupted, rattling the bottles in the cellar. The Godon faction — which included his brother and his father — gained the decisive edge and the Marchands retreated to the backyard. They regrouped, then made a second assault but were repelled.

With Godon and his allies victorious, Fawcett suddenly remembered that he did have some whiskey in the cellar. The chairs were righted and the guests settled down. About an hour later, however, Godon went outside to clear his head and found young Benjamin in the backyard. Thinking the youth was organizing another attack on the house, he dragged him inside. Godon, who towered over Marchand, knocked him down several times and then, with his opponent lying helpless on the floor, seized an axe and struck him on the head with the back of the blade.

One man tried to intervene but before he could come between Godon and his victim, Godon struck Marchand a fatal blow with the blade. Since there was neither doctor nor police closer than Fort Garry 95 km (60 miles) to the north, Fawcett went to the nearby headquarters of the Canadian Boundary Commission. He returned with a party of fifteen men led by Sergeant James H. Armstrong of the Royal Engineers. Benjamin Marchand died shortly after their arrival.

Godon surrendered quietly and was held overnight. But when the officer in charge of the Boundary Commission refused to accept responsibility for detaining him, he was released and immediately fled across the border into Dakota Territory.

Meanwhile, a coroner's jury returned a verdict that Marchand had died at the hand of Gilbert Godon. On November 12, 1873, a grand jury brought in a true bill of murder against him. When he did not appear to answer the charge, a bench warrant was issued for his arrest. But issuing a warrant was far easier than serving it. In the early days of the West, there was little co-operation between law enforcement authorities in Manitoba and Dakota Territory. There simply weren't enough policemen on either side of the line to permit the luxury of outlaw hunting. Wanted men fled either north or south of the border and as long as they remained peaceable were safe.

Unfortunately for Godon, remaining peaceful proved impossible. He was involved in a fight six months after arriving in Dakota Territory and thrown in Pembina jail just south of the border. When Manitoba's Chief Constable Richard Power learned of this development, he left for the U.S. The American lawmen were quite willing to relinquish their prisoner, and after several days hard travelling Power returned to Winnipeg with the murder suspect. The same day, June 19, 1874, Godon was arraigned and pleaded not guilty.

The communities of Dufferin, below in 1876, and Emerson in 1874.

Frontier justice moved swiftly. The following Monday he was tried for murder. After a jury deliberation of only thirty minutes, he was found guilty and sentenced to hang on August 26. A reporter at the trial described Godon as being ". . . about 22 years of age, 6' 2" in height and stout in proportion. Taken on the whole his face is rather unprepossessing. His forehead is what might be called massive, his eyes sunk deeply into his head and his whole features are devoid of expression. Throughout the whole trial he paid little attention and when the death sentence was passed he simply yawned, stretched himself as though tired of sitting in the dock and announced himself ready to go back to his cell."

He shared the death cell with Joseph Michaud, a twenty-three-year-old gunner of the Dominion Artillery. Michaud was due to hang on August 24 for the stabbing death of a passerby who had tried to intervene in a fight between a drink-crazed Michaud and another soldier.

Godon had the sympathy of at least one man. Pride of the West owner Dugald Sinclair, whose life Godon had saved in 1870, began a campaign to obtain clemency for his young friend. In response to petitions, the Canadian government commuted Godon's sentence to fourteen years imprisonment. Cellmate Michaud was not so fortunate. He was hanged in public at Winnipeg in August 1874, with so many citizens wanting to see the event that many were unable to obtain tickets.

(Although Michaud probably was not impressed, his was the first public execution carried out under the jurisdiction of the Dominion of Canada. Previously, in the days of the Hudson's Bay Company rule, a company clerk had been executed at Fort Ellice for killing an Indian. On September 6, 1845, a Salteaux Indian was publicly hanged on a makeshift gallows on the walls of Fort Garry for the murder of two Indians at the Post. Thomas Scott, the third man executed prior to Canada joining the West, had faced a Metis firing squad at Fort Garry on March 4, 1870, on warrant of the provisional government headed by Louis Riel. See Frontier booklet: *Hanging in Canada — A Concise History of a Controversial Topic.*)

After Godon's sentence was commuted he was transferred to the provincial penitentiary at Upper Fort Garry. Although he seemed resigned to serving his long sentence he was merely biding his time. On the morning of September 25, 1876, he suddenly broke from his place at the wood pile where he was working and ran towards a small boat moored on the nearby Red River. Despite a rapid volley from surprised prison guards, he escaped unscathed into the woods on the east bank.

News travelled slowly in the sparsely settled community — there being neither telephone nor telegraph — and Godon had no difficulty in collecting his horse and his wife. He again fled into Dakota Territory. By October 10, the official search for him had been given up.

For nearly a year the young outlaw flitted between Pembina and his brother's home at Emerson just north of the boundary. He was reasonably safe. On the Canadian side there were only a few provincial policemen, while on the American side no lawman was going to look for a Canadian desperado unless there was a suitable reward. But on August 18, 1877, word reached F.T. Bradley, Justice of the Peace at Emerson, that

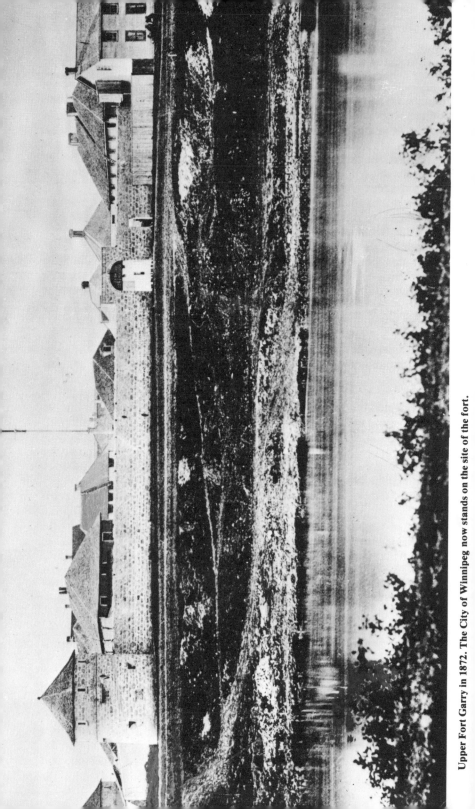

Upper Fort Garry in 1872. The City of Winnipeg now stands on the site of the fort.

Godon was planning to visit his brother. Bradley deputized brothers William and John Lucas, and sent them with his bailiff, Williams, to attempt an arrest.

At Emerson, William Lucas, in command of the miniature posse, posted the bailiff to guard a side entrance to David Godon's log house and his brother to watch the front door. Then William burst into the house — to find himself confronted by the wanted man, a loaded revolver in each hand. Before William could react, Godon's mother and sister-in-law launched themselves on him and while he warded off the blows and kicks of the screaming women, Godon slipped quickly through the side door, surprising and disarming the bailiff. He tossed the posseman's rifle into a clump of bushes and walked nonchalantly towards dense underbrush flanking the river.

Hearing the commotion, John Lucas rounded the corner of the house just as Godon began to walk away. He raised his revolver and pulled the trigger. The gun failed to fire. Then William, free of the women, fired four shots at the fugitive. He missed. At this point F.T. Bradley and another man raced up in a buggy. By the time they readied their rifles, the outlaw was beyond range.

Months passed with no word of the fugitive. Then in late February 1880, Godon's passion for drinking and brawling again betrayed him. During a drinking party at Pembina he became involved in a dispute with Alexander Montreault and broke five of his ribs. Godon was arrested by the Dakota police on a charge of assault with intent to kill, and lodged in Pembina's log prison.

Godon shared the crude frontier lock-up with two men — Frank Larose, charged with poisoning his wife, and T.P. Murray, a lightning-rod salesman held on charges of fraud and embezzlement. The three spent their days cutting wood with a bucksaw for the pot-bellied stoves in the lock-up and their evenings planning an escape. As part of the plan, they smuggled a used bucksaw blade into their cells.

The opportunity came on the night of June 25, 1880. The night watchman fell ill and had to go home. Before a replacement could be sent to the prison, the three men had unearthed the bucksaw blade, sawn a section in the ceiling and pulled themselves into the office above. From there it was a simple matter to force the front door and walk into the night. The small settlement at 3 a.m. was deserted and the men made their way undetected to an Indian camp on the Red River. Finding several unattended canoes, they stole two and paddled away.

Murray, seeking Canadian sanctuary, paddled to Winnipeg. Here he loudly protested his innocence of the charges against him in the United States. He also forsook his job as lightning-rod salesman and became a successful and respected real estate dealer in the community.

Meanwhile Godon, now wanted on both sides of the border, fled westward with Frank Larose. Some five months later a fragmentary report indicated that Godon and Larose had reached the sanctuary of a half-breed camp on the Missouri River but that Larose died shortly after their arrival of exposure and hunger. Of Gilbert Godon, the Canadian West's first indigenous outlaw, nothing more is known.

A chance encounter with a wandering prairie photographer in 1887 proved catastrophic for halfbreeds

Gaddy and Racette

James Gaddy, a slightly built halfbreed from the Crooked Lake Reserve, already had a police record when he teamed up with Moise Racette in the early summer of 1887. In addition to minor scrapes with the law, he had served a five-year sentence at Stony Mountain Penitentiary in Manitoba for horse stealing. He was released early for good behaviour, and went back to the reserve in 1884.

Moise Racette was a strong muscular man of 26 when released from the same penitentiary in April 1887. He returned to his home a little north of Wolseley, Saskatchewan. A month later, however, the pair had made contact and together gravitated to Qu'Appelle. They worked at odd jobs when they felt inclined but were always short of money. It was at Qu'Appelle that they had their photographs taken in the tent studio of Allen Sutherland, a photographer from Winnipeg. This whim was later to have disastrous consequences for the pair.

At the time, however, they were not concerned about the future. They had other problems, the main one being a lack of money to pay for the

Gaddy and Racette, opposite, await execution in Regina.
Below is Fort Qu'Appelle where the pair had their
photo taken in 1887 with disastrous consequences.

prints when they were ready. To solve their chronic lack of funds, Gaddy suggested that they obtain arms and go on a horse-stealing expedition. Racette liked the idea and they worked long enough to earn money for two revolvers.

Their next concern was horses. The pair travelled westward to Moose Jaw and stole two ponies and a black mare. Two nights later, on the return trip to Qu'Appelle, they stole a horse from homesteader Hector McLeish.

When he discovered his loss, McLeish, a tall Scot renowned for his strength, enlisted the help of his neighbor and the two started tracking the thieves. At Qu'Appelle, they were joined by Sergeant Tyffe of the NWMP and several citizens. Splitting up, the posse trailed the stolen horse towards Wolseley. From settlers along the way they obtained a good description of the horses thieves and a positive identification was made of Moise Racette.

The posse arrived at Wolseley around 10.30 p.m. on May 30. After a conference with NWMP Constable Mathewson, most of the men retired for the night at Pritchard's Hotel. McLeish and Mathewson, however, decided to continue to the Racette home 1.6 km (1 mile) north of Wolseley and stand guard during the night. They were to be joined by the posse the following morning.

Shortly after they arrived, Moise Racette left the house to saddle his horse in preparation for further flight. McLeish and Constable Mathewson conferred hastily and decided to capture Racette without assistance. Advancing, the constable placed his hand on Racette's arm and pronounced him under arrest. Racette offered no resistance.

Unaware of the policeman's presence, James Gaddy came out of the house and headed towards the corral. Big Hector McLeish stepped from his hiding place to intercept him. Unfortunately, neither McLeish nor Mathewson noticed a third man slip from the cabin's darkened doorway. His presence went undetected until he suddenly flung himself on the constable's back. Racette joined in the attack, knocking Mathewson's revolver away.

As McLeish moved in to help, Gaddy scooped up the fallen pistol and fired three times, hitting McLeish with each shot. When the melee subsided, Mathewson and the third man (who proved to be Racette's father) carried the fatally wounded McLeish into the cabin. In the meantime, Gaddy and Racette worked out a plan to murder the constable. Moise would take Mathewson with him on the pretence of going to Wolseley for a doctor. At a given signal, he would fling himself to the ground so that Gaddy could shoot the policeman.

The plan would have worked except that in the darkness Gaddy missed with his first shot. Mathewson spun off the trail, grappling with Racette as two more shots grazed his uniform. He was soon overpowered by the outlaws but for some reason their plan to kill the constable was abandoned and they returned with him to the Racette cabin. There, after warning him not to leave until they had gone, they saddled their stolen horses and rode away.

As soon as the sound of their horses faded. Mathewson ran for help. A doctor was quickly at the scene and arranged for McLeish to go to Wolseley, but the big Scot died at 8.40 that morning in the hotel.

For the next few days angry armed posses of settlers and police surrounded the Crooked Lake Reserve and searched every foot of it. Gaddy and Racette hid out with various friends and, eluding the cordon, headed south through the Cypress Hills into Montana.

Once across the "Medicine Line" as the Indians called the border, they changed their names. Gaddy worked on a sheep ranch while Racette joined a semi-nomadic band of Montana halfbreeds. He soon married one of the girls.

Meanwhile, photographer Allen Sutherland had completed his summer tour and returned to Winnipeg. Here he read of the murder and the descriptions of the wanted men. Struck by the resemblance between the outlaws and the two men who had been unable to pay for their photographs earlier that summer, he contacted Lieutenant-Governor Dewdney. When the photographs proved to be of Gaddy and Racette, Dewdney puchased a dozen for $5 and sent them to the Mounted Police. Since the police were reasonably certain that the two outlaws were in northern Montana, they forwarded copies of the photograph to Indian agents, army officers and sheriffs in the area. Weeks passed without results.

Then on July 18, Gaddy, Racette and another man named Leroy were seen near Fort Ellice on the Canadian side of the line. A posse was quickly assembled but after two days of hard riding they discovered that the three men had separated and effectively covered their trails.

There followed another long wait, but on August 12 the photographs again assisted the lawmen. Sheriff Beck of Lewiston, Montana, noticed two men at the army post of Fort McGinnis and was positive that they were Gaddy and Racette. Assisted by W.H. Simons, he surprised and arrested them. Word was sent by telegraph to the NWMP at Regina.

Mathewson, now promoted to Corporal, the Crown Prosecutor, and a settler from Wolseley went to Fort McGinnis where they identified both men. By November, Gaddy and Racette were lodged in the NWMP cells at Regina. Sheriff Beck and Simons shared the $500 reward.

A preliminary hearing resulted in a trial date, set for January 10, 1888. However, owing to a defence counsel request for an opinion on James Gaddy's "soundness of mind," the trial was postponed for four weeks to February 6.

Court was held at Wolseley on that date with Mr. Justice Wetmore presiding. A surprise Crown witness was Peter Gaddy, James' brother, who testified that he had seen the entire episode on the night of the McLeish murder. His testimony, as well as that of numerous other witnesses, clinched the Crown's case. Both were convicted and sentenced to death. From the same cell-block that had housed the famous Louis Riel, Gaddy and Racette were led to the scaffold on June 13, 1888.

A grimly humorous footnote was added in 1894. Photographer Allen Sutherland visited the Crooked Lake Reserve that summer and was attracted to an aged Indian whose face he thought would make an excellent portrait. To his surprise, the man refused to pose. Sutherland later learned that the old Indian didn't want his picture taken "by the machine that hung Gaddy and Racette."

Henry Wagner: Merciless Killer

**In darkness illuminated by flashes from a six-gun
fired by a killer who had just murdered a police officer,
an unarmed rookie policeman fought what has been described
as ". . . one of the greatest, man-to-man battles in
Western police history."**

**The post office-store in Union Bay
on Vancouver Island where
Wagner committed his last murder.**

38

Darkness eerily shrouded the little coal-shipping town of Union Bay, Vancouver Island, on the night of March 4, 1913. It was shortly before midnight and a southeast wind moaned in from the Gulf of Georgia and made the darkness more sombre and ominous. The only bright spot was the saloon, where a score of miners and dock employees sipped their beer and toddy and seemed loth to leave the snug shelter of the place.

"Time to close, gentlemen," announced the bartender, herding his reluctant patrons to the doorway, and bidding them goodnight.

The men shivered as they strode out into the dark of the night.

"Swell night for a murder," announced one with a shudder as he pulled his coat collar about his ears.

"Sure is," agreed a companion, bending his head to the wind.

Little did the two realize that they were speaking prophetically. At that moment Death was arranging the stage for a tragedy that would result in a police officer dying and his killer hanging from a gallows.

"Wonder if the ghost prowler will work tonight," said the first man, striding along the dark road beside his friend.

A grunt was the only reply. The man who voiced the inquiry was not alone in his wondering. Several hundred men and women of the town had

spoken the same words to each other as they prepared to retire.

Another who asked himself the same question was "Big Mac," officially known as Provincial Constable J. McKenzie, as he patrolled in the darkness. Big Mac was a good policeman and had proved his bravery time and again, when, unarmed, he quelled incipient riots and drunken brawls among the miners, dockworkers and sailors. But the "ghost prowler" had him baffled.

For weeks now the elusive prowler had entered stores and dwellings, selected his loot and departed without being seen. What he did with his plunder was another question. None of it appeared in the usual channel chosen by thieves for disposal of stolen goods.

If McKenzie was watching a store at one end of the small town, the prowler would select one at the other. Apparently he knew the officer and watched his movements. No matter what ruse the policeman tried he was always outwitted.

Since McKenzie knew every man, woman and child in Union Bay and the surrounding towns and settlements he had eliminated them all from possible connection with the robberies. The thing was uncanny. How could a human prowler gain entry to place after place without being seen by someone and then leave no clue as to his identity?

McKenzie was discouraged but he had a streak of Scottish stubborness and continued to maintain his night guard over stores that he thought might be entered. If the prowler was human he would capture him, he swore. It was bad enough to be outwitted, but now citizens were beginning to criticize him.

While the events which worried McKenzie were happening, two "rookie Cops" were undergoing training under the tutorship of Provincial Constable David Stephenson at Nanaimo. They were Constable Harry Westaway, an adventure-seeking lad from Eastern Canada, and Constable Gordon Ross, who had enlisted in his native Scotland for service in the South African War and later immigrated to Canada. Meeting by chance, the young men enlisted in the police force in search of further adventure.

Stephenson knew McKenzie for an efficient and conscientious officer and did not blame him for the failure to make an arrest. "New methods must be tried," the chief muttered as he scanned McKenzie's latest report on the prowler's activities, and sent for Ross and Westaway.

"I am going to assign you men to special duty," the Chief announced. "You may have heard of the looting of stores and dwellings at Union Bay. It has to be stopped and I am going to give you lads a chance to do the stopping.

"Whoever is responsible for these robberies seems to keep a careful watch on the officer there and breaks into one place while another is being guarded.

"I am casting no reflection on McKenzie. He is a splendid man, but I think it wise to send men who are not known in Union Bay. It is to be expected that the robber or robbers will attempt to loot the big general store in which the post office is located. As yet it has not been touched.

"The postmaster is the only person in Union Bay who knows of my plans. McKenzie knows nothing of them. Go to the postmaster and he will

40

furnish you with a key to the store and you two will stand guard in the place from midnight to dawn every day.

"Allow no person to see you enter the store and by all means never be seen in company with McKenzie or disclose your identity to him until after everything is cleaned up. If you are seen with him it might be suspected that you are police officers.

"It might be best for you to pose as men seeking work, but you may use your own judgment. I warn you that I do not want you to fail."

The assignment was accepted with pleasure by the two young men. Freedom from tiresome routine duty with a prospect of high adventure was something to be appreciated. Kits were soon packed and the rookies were on their way, eagerly talking over their prospects for success.

Two days following receipt of their assignment they were registered at Union Bay's best hotel and let inquiring loafers know that while they were temporarily in funds they would not pass up any opportunity for employment. They were told that work was hard to get but there was a possibility of new hands being taken on at docks and mines in the near future. The news was just the kind the officers hoped to hear. "We'll stick around then," they declared.

McKenzie, ever on the alert, did not fail to notice the arrival of the newcomers. He questioned them but dismissed them as young men genuinely in search of work.

Meanwhile, the sleuths had obtained the key to the store and post office and each night stole into the building and kept vigil. One would sleep on the counter for a few hours while the other stood guard, unarmed except for a police "billy."

Westaway had produced a broken-down, small revolver and shown it to his comrade when the vigil started. "For Pete's sake put it away," Ross said. "It's more dangerous to the man who shoots it than it is to the man who is shot at."

His companion laughed and tossed the weapon into his kit bag.

The assignment was proving to be quite a holiday for the pair. Nothing came of their vigils. True, other places were broken into and looted, but those cases were not their problem — they belonged to the baffled McKenzie.

Then came the night of March 4. Westaway noticed something wrong as they entered the building. In the post office section, a blind which should have been pulled down according to arrangements made with the postmaster was slighty raised and allowed a shaft of light from the nearby hotel to enter. Silently indicating to Ross what he considered the postmaster's oversight, Westaway moved to pull down the blind while Ross continued to the door leading to the store.

Just as Ross passed through the portal he heard a board creak. Bending low, he peered into the store and called to Westaway. "There is someone in here!"

"Coming," said Westaway, turning away from the window.

"Hold up your hands or I'll shoot," commanded Ross, still peering toward the source of the sound.

The light coming through the window below the slightly raised blind

Gordon Ross in later years when he was a detective with the Vancouver Police Department.

The "Flying Dutchman" when he was behind bars at Walla Walla in Washington State. Below is Union Bay's Wilson Hotel in 1908 where the two police officers stayed.

reduced the darkness of the store to some extent. Suddenly Ross discerned two faces peering at him from behind the end of a long counter. There was something else. He saw the ugly muzzle of a big revolver pointed in his direction.

Ignoring the threat of the revolver, Ross hurled himself at the two men just as Westaway rushed through the door to join him in danger.

The heavy revolver exploded. "I'm hit!" gasped Westaway.

Ross heard Westaway's cry but continued his mad plunge and grabbed the gunman. Cans, crockery and hardware crashed to the floor as one man fought for the revolver while the other struggled to retain it.

Westaway gamely endeavored to assist Ross but suddenly collapsed across his comrade's legs and all three men fell to the floor.

"There's another man in the store. Get him," called Ross as he attempted to seize his opponent's throat. He found his grip but lost it when the powerful muscles beneath his fingers suddenly swelled.

Ross tried again, but his antagonist's teeth seized two of his fingers. He heard a crunch and felt an agonizing pain as teeth met bone. Then the officer remembered the billy in his pocket and managed to drag it out. Again and again he struck and had the satisfaction of hearing the weapon thud on flesh and bone. Then, without warning, his opponent went limp. Ross relaxed. It was a fatal error. His adversary gave a mighty heave and tossed Ross to one side, the billy flying from his hand.

Ross tried to protect himself from blows rained on him with a revolver. One blow struck him on the shoulder, the next landed on his head. Barely conscious, Ross became aware that the gunman had lost his weapon. The battle continued, each man attempting to pick up the fallen revolver as they weltered in their own blood and that of the wounded Westaway. Suddenly Ross felt his club beneath him as he rolled on the floor, locked in the gunman's grip. Could he reach and seize the weapon?

Desperately taking a chance, he grabbed for the club. The balance of the battle changed. Without mercy, Ross pounded his adversary until the man displayed no signs of resistance. Even then he struck several more blows before he attempted to handcuff his captive. The handcuffs were of an old type and he only succeeded in securing them on one wrist before the other cuff locked.

Dragging his unconscious prisoner by the handcuffs he searched for his fellow officer and stumbled over Westaway's legs. Westaway had managed to crawl painfully until he was almost at the front of the store, only to collapse partly under a table. Stirring feebly, he murmured, "Goodbye, Gordon, I'm gone."

"You'll be all right and I've got the man who shot you," assured Ross.

His statement was never heard by his pal. Westaway was dead.

Sick with pain, weak from loss of blood and crazed by the death of Westaway, Ross was on the verge of collapse. For the moment he hoped that his blows had brought death to the man who had fired the shot that killed Westaway. But this hope was shattered when the captive stirred and seemed about to resume the struggle. Ross slugged him viciously until his body was again limp and lifeless.

Ross was in a predicament. He was afraid to leave his prisoner, and was so weak himself he thought he might collapse at any minute. With what strength he had he hurled the club at the glass in the door in hope that someone would come to the rescue.

Why no one heard the shot that killed Westaway puzzled him. Ross would have been even more puzzled had he realized that there had been six shots, not one. The prowler had emptied his revolver in a vain attempt to kill him. Ross's body was seared by flame from the pistol, but this fact he did not discover until later.

The shots, however, had been heard by Constable McKenzie. But the building muffled them and he could not discover their source. That they came from the post office was the last possibility and he was making his way there when the quiet was shattered by the crash of glass.

McKenzie broke into a run. Reaching the post office, he hurled himself against the door. "Stick up your hands and stand still or I'll shoot," he bluffed, for he was not armed. The figure of a man appeared in the darkness. McKenzie gasped. The face he looked into was hardly a face at all. Battered, bruised and bloody, it gibbered through swollen lips. "I'm a police officer. This man killed my pal and I got him."

Looking down, McKenzie saw that the figure was dragging at the end of a pair of handcuffs a man just as bruised and bloody. Farther along the floor lay another man, deathly still, in a pool of blood.

Ross submitted to being searched by McKenzie, who was satisfied when he discovered a Provincial Police badge in his pocket. "Guess you are all right," he said. "What happened?"

From Ross's slurred account he made out that another prowler was still in the store.

"Wait here and don't move," McKenzie ordered, and set out to search the dark store. It did not take him long to satisfy himself that the second prowler had escaped by leaping through a window, probably after the first shot was fired. He returned to the front of the store and lit a large lamp. The scene was one of devastation. One man dead, two battered almost beyond description, and blood everywhere — the floor, walls, counters and shelves. Cans, bottles and crockery littered the floor.

McKenzie examined the prostrate Westaway as Ross told him something of the story. The bullet had entered in the region of Westaway's heart and he had bled badly. Only pluck had kept him going so long after being hit.

Searching the premises, McKenzie found bandages and water and bound Ross's wounds. When this first aid was done he noticed that the prisoner was stirring. Quickly he fettered him with handcuffs. "Can you stay with him while I get help?" McKenzie asked Ross. "Chief Stephenson is at Cumberland and if I can get a phone call through I will have him over."

It seemed hours before McKenzie returned with Stephenson who after expressing sorrow over Westaway's fate, listened to Ross tell his story until they were interrupted by the prisoner's regaining consciousness. Stephenson knelt beside him and shook him roughly.

"Who is your partner?" he demanded.

"Bill Julian," muttered the prisoner. He groaned as he opened his eyes and blinked at the light. It was a moment before he realized he had subconsciously betrayed his accomplice to a police officer, and refused to answer further questions.

Stephenson was about to get up when he noticed a mole on the prisoner's cheek. In spite of the cuts and bruises it stood out like a brand on his battered face. "Ross, I believe you have captured the 'Flying Dutchman'!" Stephenson exclaimed.

The prisoner glared balefully as he heard this statement.

"The Flying Dutchman!" Who among Western officers had not heard of Henry Wagner, alias Harry Ferguson and a dozen other aliases, and notoriously known as "The Flying Dutchman." He was almost a mythical figure representing the last and the worst of the bad men of the Old West. Some years previous he had been chief of the infamous Cassidy gang that had terrorized Wyoming and neighboring states, a gang that had committed scores of murders, holdups and train robberies. Sheriffs' posses had failed to round up the gang and eventually U.S. authorities had sent out the hard-riding cavalry with orders to exterminate these human rats.

The soldiers did their work well. Eighteen of the outlaws were shot down, but Wagner and his henchman, Bill Julian, sought safety in flight, and continued their criminal careers. They served prison terms and in some instances escaped from custody. Each time, however, their connection with the Cassidy gang was not established until after they were free.

In attempting to rob a post office in the State of Washington, Wagner had shot and killed the postmaster. He and his aide then stole a boat called the *Spray* and began a career of crime along the B.C. coast that earned Wagner the nickname "The Flying Dutchman" because of his steal-and-disappear tactics.

Ross could hardly believe it possible until later when Stephenson showed him a circular bearing a photograph and description of the much-wanted man.

While officers were preparing to remove Wagner to the Cumberland jail, they found a clever contrivance on him. Flashlights were little known at the time, so Wagner had made his own. To a set of dry-cell batteries carried in his hip pocket, he had attached wires which led to a switch and a small light bulb that he held in his hand. The light was admirably suited for his prowling and felonious activities.

After seeing Wagner lodged in jail and the body of Westaway removed to an undertaker's, Ross left for his hotel. That afternoon he visited the jail to inspect his captive. Stephenson was there and asked Wagner: "Do you know this man?" pointing to Ross.

"Yes, I know him, but he never took me alone. He must have had help." Wagner always maintained that no one man could capture him alive.

Another policeman who examined Wagner was Constable George Hannay. He knew every inch of the coast in the area and said that he believed he had seen the prisoner and another man on a small homestead on Lasqueti Island, some distance from the Vancouver Island shore. He was sure that the other man was Julian. Hannay was given charge of the search and for several days lay in hiding on a bleak, rocky islet just off the Lasqueti Island homestead. His patience was rewarded, for he saw Julian tugging at the oars of a small boat, making his way to the homestead. He quickly took the man into custody. A search of the homestead shack resulted in recovery of most of the loot taken from Union Bay stores and houses.

Julian, desperately attempting to save his own neck, gave the police every assistance and corroborated Ross's story about events in the store when Westaway was murdered. He also talked freely of the other crimes he and his chief had committed.

Wagner and he had used a motorboat to carry them on their forays from Lasqueti Island. On the night Westaway was shot he had fled at the first gun blast, but on going to the boat found that he could not start it. Wagner, apparently not even trusting his accomplice, had removed part of the engine mechanism. Bill was compelled to flee in a small dinghy they had towed behind the launch.

Thereafter justice moved swiftly. A coroner's jury named Wagner Westaway's slayer and he was committed for trial at the Spring Assizes where Bill Julian was the prosecution's chief witness.

During Wagner's trial an officer from the State of Washington sat in the court room. Should Wagner have been acquitted he was ready to take him to Washington to stand trial for the murder of the postmaster. But there was no acquittal. The evidence was overwhelming and Wagner could offer no defence. All he could do was utter threats against Julian who had betrayed him and who was jailed for five years for his part in the crime. While Julian was happy at dodging the gallows, he trembled with fear at the possibility of Wagner escaping.

No opportunity was given the condemned man to escape punishment. He did attempt, however, to dash his brains out by beating his head against the wall as he awaited execution. This attempt only led to a closer guard being kept over him. He was even deprived of shaving material to avoid the possibility of his slashing his throat.

On August 28, 1913, Wagner faced death — a fate which he had so mercilessly meted out to others. A small crowd of spectators gathered in the prison yard at Nanaimo to see the sentence carried out. Wagner presented a wild appearance as he marched to the gallows from which the hangman's noose dangled. His hair and beard were long and unkempt. A fit he suffered the night before the execution heightened the prison pallor of his face. Reaching the foot of the gallows, he gazed up at the gibbet, then rushed up the stairs and stood beneath the noose.

Arthur Ellis, Canada's official executioner, quickly adjusted the noose as the black cap slipped over the condemned man's head. The trap was sprung just as the preacher began the Lord's Prayer. (As related on the following pages, the hanging set a new world's record for speed.)

When it was over, Constable Gordon Ross suddenly remembered it was his birthday. He had received a grim gift — the avenging of his comrade's death.

My Friend, The Hangman

In Canada from Confederation until 1976 when capital punishment was abolished, over 400 men and women were hanged. Among the hangmen was Arthur Ellis who called himself "Official Executioner to the Dominion of Canada." He hanged Dutch Wagner in world record time, with a reluctant participant the late B.A. McKelvie, one of British Columbia's best known author-historians.

Arthur Ellis, hangman for over twenty years.

Yes, I recall Arthur Ellis, for many years public executioner for the Dominion of Canada, as a friend. It is because of my liking for him that I am writing this story in order to keep a promise I made to him. This promise was made in all good faith, but the family journals for which I ordinarily wrote were not anxious to publish it, for there was a certain squeamishness among editors in running articles on hangmen.

Arthur Ellis was an artist. I like artists who take a pride in their work. Besides, he was a genial, kind-hearted little chap, always ready to alleviate distress. I've seen him cry when told of the sufferings of a poor family.

His work he regarded as purely impersonal. His was a duty to perform, and he did it. "I am an executioner (he shunned the word 'hangman' as being vulgar) because I believe that I can carry out the judgment of the law with less pain and anguish to the condemned than can any other man in the world," he once told me.

It was on this occasion which he asked me to write a story in defence of his calling.

"A murder is committed," he explained, "and the entire populace calls out for the arrest and execution of the killer. A policeman, a respected official, arrests the man. He comes before a magistrate, a man of standing in the community, who commits the accused to stand trial in the Assize Court. In due time he appears before the tribunal. Twelve of his fellow citizens, acting as a jury, weigh the evidence and pronounce him guilty of the charge upon which he has been indicted. A Justice, who is honored by all, pronounces the sentence of death.

"I carry out that sentence — and I have to go about the country under an assumed name; if a hotelman learns I'm in his house, he asks me to vacate it. I am but one cog in the machinery of justice, and I am entitled to just as much respect as the Justice of the Assize Court. It is unfair — and," he concluded shyly, "I would appreciate if you would write something in defence of my position."

He was naturally gregarious in disposition. He loved companionship, and it hurt him that men would turn away from him because they did not like his profession.

"But what chance had I," he protested. "My forefathers for 300 years were the executioners of England. It is customary there for a lad to follow in the family trade or profession — and, besides, few would consent to take the son of an executioner as an apprentice in another calling — so naturally I was trained as an executioner. I had to study for

48

twelve years before I was permitted on a scaffold. I know more about the human body than many doctors; I must be able to look at a man and judge his weight at a glance; I have to know all about stresses and strains and muscular reactions — oh, there's a great deal to learn in my profession.''

We were sitting on the marble stairs of Vancouver's police head-quarters when he gave me this authorized interview. There was a lawyer — let's call him Frank — and Arthur and I. Frank, who had an inquiring mind, started to question Arthur about the niceties of his calling. Arthur was in a responsive mood, he gave us details. He described the whole operation. He explained how he had to test the rope to stand a definite weight.

"But how do you know what the condemned man will weigh?" asked Frank.

"I take a look at him in his cell. I can tell to within a fraction of a pound his weight after one glance. You see the length of the drop depends upon the weight of the subject.

"Now, our friend here," and he indicated me, "weighs 208 pounds.'' That was my exact weight that very afternoon, and I wasn't boasting about it. "I would, ahem! — give him 4 feet, 10 inches of a drop; he would be absolutely dead in 11 minutes. Of course," he hastened to assure us, "he would be really dead to all intents and purposes as soon as he dropped, but it would take 11 minutes for his circulatory system to stop completely." So it was that Arthur gratuitously gave me a bit of information that I'll wager few people have concerning themselves.

Wagner was hanged in Nanaimo, shown here in the early 1900s. This was the era when traffic kept to the left, as shown by the right-hand drive cars.

It was all very interesting to Frank. "How do you tie the knot?" he questioned.

"I'll show you," exclaimed Arthur. He grabbed his club bag, which I naturally thought had his pyjamas and brush and comb. He opened it and displayed a fine assortment of ropes and black caps. Deftly he tied a noose. "Now," he said with mounting enthusiasm, "I'd place it right there," and he indicated a point just behind my left ear — and his cold hands rather fondly felt my neck. "I'd break the third vertebrae," he boasted. Honestly, I didn't quite like being a guinea pig for a hangman's lecture on his art. Especially so, when to further demonstrate the exactitude with which the rope should be adjusted, he wanted to put a black cap over my head and the noose about my neck. You see, recognizing the true artist in Arthur, and probably unjustly, I was just a mite afraid that in his enthusiasm and desire to fully demonstrate he might push me over the banister. I declined.

That was Arthur all over. He was an enthusiast. He was devoted to his art. In fact he was so devoted that in B.C. he established a world's record in speed for an official hanging. Although it was the first time I had ever seen him I, to my surprise, became one of the timekeepers at this hanging. The man involved was Henry Wagner, who rejoiced in the alias of "The Flying Dutchman."

It was the summer of 1913. I was sent to witness the event. It was a glorious morning. The sun was streaming into the dining-room of the Old Windsor Hotel at Nanaimo when I went down for an early breakfast. There was no one in the room as I entered. I was hardly seated when a dapper little man in a grey suit, with a pink rose in his buttonhole, bounced in and approached my table.

"May I sit here?" he questioned after giving me a cheery greeting.

"Certainly," I replied.

"You're up early this morning," he beamed.

I nodded agreement.

"Perhaps," he ventured, "you're going down to see the regrettable affair at the jail?"

"I am, unfortunately," I said.

"Ah, too bad that such things have to be," he murmured, shaking his head. "But then, men will commit crimes that the law decrees deserve capital punishment — and the law must be supported."

"I suppose so."

"Are you a commercial man?" queried my table companion.

"No, a newspaper reporter."

He fairly beamed; "Oh, I know a number of newspaper men," he volunteered.

From that introduction we drifted into a discussion of literature, and I found that the pleasant stranger was a great admirer of Browning. Suddenly he looked at his watch. "Oh," he exclaimed, "I must be off." He bounced out of the room, turning at the door to smile, "I'll see you later."

When I stepped through the little door into the high-walled courtyard of the jail, to my surprise the first man I saw was my friend of the breakfast table. He rushed up to me. "You didn't know you had the honor of breakfasting with the public executioner," he said.

"I certainly did not!"

"Well," he chattered on without noting the chill in my reply, "I have a favor to ask of you."

I shuddered.

"This is the first time I have performed the execution of my duty on the Pacific Coast," he continued, and I took mental note of the appropriateness of the word "Execution."

"I find conditions here are identical with those under which my uncle established a world's record in executions in England in 1887," he said. "I'm out to establish a new world record. You see this police constable. He has a stop watch. I want you to stand beside him and see that the instant the condemned man's foot touches gravel when he comes through that door that the watch starts, and that it stops the second the trap is sprung."

The request was such a relief to what I expected he was going to ask me to do that I consented.

Then Arthur ran up on the scaffold. He faced the grim little crowd, rubbing his hands together and smiling agreeably. "Gentlemen," he said. "This is a wonderful country you have out here — and such glorious weather! This is the first time that I have visited you and as conditions are similar to those when my uncle established a world's record in executions, I am hoping to break that record today to celebrate the first time I have visited the Pacific Coast.

"Now, gentlemen," he said, growing serious, "when the condemned man appears you will kindly lift your hats — not necessarily out of respect for him, but for the law.

"Usually it is the custom to screen the foot of the scaffold so that you cannot see the condemned man after he disappears through the trap, but owing to the fact that this is my first time here and I am hoping to establish a new record, I have left the screen off, so you can see everything."

Just then the door opened. As the Flying Dutchman's foot touched the ground I saw the watch hand move.

Accompanied by a Salvation Army officer and the sheriff, he moved across the yard to the ramp that reached to the scaffold. I glanced at Arthur. He was crouched inward, a black cap in one hand and a leg strap in the other.

As they reached the trap, Arthur sprang into action. There was a black flash as the cap went on and, almost at the same time, the strap went about the Dutchman's legs. The Salvation Army officer had only time to murmur the first three or four words of the Lord's Prayer when the trap was sprung. Almost before the rope tightened, Arthur, with hand uplifted, shouted, "Time."

"Forty-seven seconds," answered the constable, and he was correct.

"Gentlemen, gentlemen," beamed proud Arthur, again rubbing his hands, "you have been privileged to witness 11 seconds clipped from the record set by my uncle. You have seen a new world's record in hanging."

And that's how I first met my friend, the hangman.

This short man with iron fists became the first chief of police in Winnipeg, Calgary and Rossland. He was also Western Canada's first police chief convicted of being a customer in a Winnipeg bawdyhouse.

The West's Wandering Police Chief

The little province of Manitoba that joined Canada on July 15, 1870, would have qualified anywhere in the world as a rough, tough community. Brawls, violence and alcohol were part of its way of life. The metropolis of this first unit of "civilization" west of Toronto was Winnipeg.

Winnipeg was a rugged town. It had twenty-eight saloons and brothels — famous among which were the Red Saloon whose proprietor was killed in a fight; the Prairie Saloon, which boasted the cleanest dirt floor in the community; and Dugald Sinclair's Pride of the West

John S. Ingram, and
Winnipeg in 1874, the year
of its incorporation.

emporium, sometimes called "The Bucket of Blood" because of the frequent barroom brawls. Main Street, usually a quagmire of mud, was fronted by places of business catering to a gaudy parade of fur traders, frontiersmen, half-breeds and Indians, while the prairie behind was dotted with tents, shacks and shanties housing the human flotsam and jetsam of any frontier outpost.

Main Street petered out on the prairie. Beyond the last dust-soiled tent was a no-man's land where life was cheap and the only law that of the bullet or the knife Apart from a few isolated settlements such as Portage la Prairie, Fort Ellice and Fort Edmonton, the white man had made little, if any, impact on the land of the Indian.

Law enforcement in such a sparsely populated territory had its problems. For example, in early August 1875 word was sent to Winnipeg that the sheriff at Portage la Prairie was holding a Sioux Indian and six confederates on suspicion of murdering another Indian. There being neither jail, handcuffs nor leg irons, the prisoners were placed under guard in a shed on the sheriff's farm.

When coroner Dr. Cowan arrived from Winnipeg in his buggy, he found the entire male population of Portage la Prairie on guard duty. In order to carry out his duties properly, Dr. Cowan had to borrow most of the guards to make up a jury, with the result that the seven prisoners overpowered the remaining guards and escaped.

Although this sequence of events was embarrassing to the sheriff and other local authorities, it had been topped the previous month in Winnipeg. There the City Council had accepted their police chief's resignation after he had been found in a brothel — but not on official business.

The chief was John S. Ingram, a short powerfully built man of twenty-three who was fond of wine, women and cigars. He arrived in Winnipeg in 1873, an argumentative type prone to settling disputes with his fists. Despite his pugnacious manner, he was to survive three tempestuous decades until a tragic day in far-off British Columbia.

Shortly after his arrival in Winnipeg, he joined the small police force and rose to prominence by successfully arresting the popular Ambroise Lepine, an ex-Louis Riel follower accused of complicity in the execution of Thomas Scott in March 1870. (During the Riel Uprising, Scott had been executed publicly by a firing squad for activities against the Riel-headed government. After Riel's illegal government was dismantled later the same year, warrants were issued for the arrests of those connected with the execution.)

From this success, Ingram passed on to other triumphs. When Winnipeg was incorporated in 1874, he became its first chief of police. While his jurisdiction did not extend beyond the town, it covered a wide variety of duties. Among them was night watchman, dog catcher, licence issuer, saloon bouncer, and miscellaneous other functions imposed by city council, including ensuring that sidewalks were kept free of snow.

Shortly after John Ingram's appointment as chief of police, temptation reared in the form of a bevy of girls who arrived from Ontario under the guidance of Madame Carrie Lyons. Ella Lewis, Fannie J. Ellsworth, Carrie Rowland, Nellie Foster and Addie Booth had the questionable distinction of being the first professional prostitutes on the new frontier. Madame Lyons set up quarters in the west end of town and opened for business.

Not long afterward rumors began to circulate that the youthful Chief Ingram was a nightly visitor to these houses of ill-fame and that his presence was not official. The rumors proved true the following spring when Ingram's two constables, Byers and Murray, resigned in protest over the conduct of the force. The City Council refused to accept their resignations and Alderman John Villiers publicly accused Ingram of operating a primitive system of protection and using his authority to hide his participation in the vices of the west end. Ingram retaliated by filing a $10,000 libel suit against Villiers. But he also continued his unofficial visits to establishments such as Madame Carrie's.

At least he did until a night in June 1875 when Constables Murray and Byers swooped down on a sin-bin operated by Ella Lewis and arrested Ingram as one of the "found-ins."

Next morning a red-faced police chief appeared before the local magistrate and paid a fine of $8 and costs. Ingram quickly left for his home town of St. Thomas, Ontario, the libel suit discreetly forgotten. An even redder-faced city council accepted his resignation and appointed Murray to succeed him as chief.

After an appropriate interval, Ingram returned to Winnipeg. Although he appeared from time to time in magistrate's court for

A Winnipeg saloon in the early 1880s.

practising his favorite pastime of pugilism, he made no further mark upon the community. When the CPR began to snake its way westward across the prairies in the early 1880s, Ingram followed the newly laid rails.

In 1884, the recently incorporated city of Calgary was searching for a man to head its new police force. Up to that point police duties had been handled by the local North-West Mounted Police detachment. There were four applicants for the position and after the ballots were counted at the January 7, 1885, council meeting, John S. Ingram emerged as the new chief of police. While there were raised eyebrows from those who knew Ingram's reputation for brawling and womanizing, there was little question that the council had chosen well. Calgary, hub of a network of rail and stagecoach lines, was the mecca for every gambler, ruffian and horse thief in the country. Wranglers like Crackerbox Bill and Bulldog Kelly strutted the streets; gamblers like Jumbo Fisk skulked in the back rooms of the hotels; confidence men like Scott Krenger preyed on the greedy and the innocent; while ladies of the night like Nina Dow and

Rossland in 1897 when Ingram was its first chief of police.

Maud Lewis gathered the lonely to their bosoms. A strong man was required to maintain any semblance of order and supply some protection for the budding cow town aristocracy.

No gunman, Chief Ingram relied on speed and his fists to keep order. A brawler of repute in a time when most arguments were settled by hand-to-nose combat, he prowled the streets, cigar clenched between teeth, official hat tilted on his head. Shunned by the elite of the town, tolerated by members of city council, he made few friends and many enemies but kept Calgary lawful.

Once or twice he planted a fist in the wrong place, but in an age when a bartender would shoot a customer for taking two cigars while only paying for one, Ingram walked a tightrope between dictatorship and anarchy. With only two constables to assist him, he operated from the back room of a billiard hall on Stephen Avenue and by sheer force of personality dominated the criminal element. When he married Edith Oake of Hyde, England, in October 1887, the boys threw an all night party for him.

One of Ingram's enemies was the editor of the powerful Calgary newspaper, *The Herald*. After a three-year reign along the wooden sidewalks, Ingram bowed to the steady campaign pressure against him and handed in his resignation in February 1888. Despite his rough and ready methods, the stocky man with fists of iron had protected the foothills cow town. Soon after his departure a circle of petty thieves and bold prostitutes led by May Buchanan kept the town in a turmoil.

For a time after leaving the force, John Ingram operated the Palace and Royal Hotels in Calgary, then moved to Great Falls, Montana. In 1896 he fortuitously turned up in Rossland, British Columbia, which was in the throes of incorporation. In April 1897 he was chosen its first chief of police. Thirteen years had not mellowed Ingram and for the next four years he ruled vigorously. He resigned in 1901 when a man with whom he had disagreed was elected mayor. He served again in 1902-03, but finally retired in 1904 with another change of civic slate.

Still a relatively young man of fifty-two, Ingram went to work for the Centre Star Mining Company as dynamite man — a job even more hazardous than confronting armed criminals. Shortly after noon on a December day in 1905, Ingram was preparing fuses in the fuse room. A few feet away in the powder room dynamite was thawing. There was a sudden flash of flame, followed by a massive explosion. Death, which had been Ingram's constant companion as a peace officer, came suddenly and violently to the man with the iron fists.

When rescuers arrived they found only a gaping hole where the powder house and fuse room had been. Ingram's body was some distance away. He was the only fatality in an explosion that injured twenty and caused $50,000 damage.

On December 20, 1905, John S. Ingram, first chief of police in the West, was placed aboard a train for his last ride home. Said the *Rossland Miner:* "John had the good qualities and the faults of most strong men. He was a firm and enduring friend to those he liked and a relentless enemy of those he hated."

Calgary's First Hanging

Minutes after cutting his victim's throat Jess Williams was under arrest. He subsequently became the first non-Indian hanged in the three million-square-mile Northwest Territories.

Malcolm McNeil stopped the bay team in front of McKelvie's Store in the newly born foothills community of Calgary and threw the reins to his companions. Promising not to keep them waiting long in the crisp February night, he slid from the sleigh seat, rubbed some circulation back into his chilled limbs and walked across the sidewalk covered with new-fallen snow. It was 8:30 on the evening of Friday, February 8, 1884.

A little bell tinkled gently as he opened the door of the grocery store, but there was no sign of life. McNeil unbuttoned his heavy sheepskin coat as he walked to the counter. "Mr. McKelvie?" There was no answer.

McNeil looked around the store. "Jim Adams?" Then he saw the

Inspector T. Dowling was in charge of the investigation. Below is Calgary's Stephen Avenue in 1884.

crumpled figure behind the counter.

"Jim! Sleeping on the job? What will old man McKelvie . . . ." McNeil stopped short, gripped by terror. The head of the man he thought was asleep lay in a pool of blood.

McNeil spun back to the door. "Spearon! Hogg! Come in here. Jim's hurt himself!"

His two hunting companions joined him to stare in disbelief at the scene. Then with a natural distrust of death and violence that most men possess, the trio backed slowly to the doorway. As they did a man named Fraser who operated a confectionary store adjacent to the grocery pushed

59

through the door. "What's going on here," he demanded. "Somebody said Jim Adams was hurt."

"See for yourself," McNeil pointed to the body of the young man. "Jim's done himself in."

Fraser looked at the body. One glance was enough to see the gaping wound in the men's neck. "Incredible," he muttered. "He was in my store just half an hour ago to borrow a pitcher of water for his tea. Chipper as a squirrel. Well, we'd better get the police."

When the report of the suicide came into the North-West Mounted Police at Calgary, Inspector Sam Steele detailed Inspector Tom Dowling and Dr. Kennedy to investigate. Arriving at the McKelvie store they discovered that a group of citizens had already gathered and that the affair had taken a different turn. What at first looked like a simple case of suicide was obviously cold-blooded murder.

While Dr. Kennedy knelt to examine the still warm body, Inspector Dowling questioned those present. From store owner McKelvie, hastily summoned from a church meeting, he learned that the victim was a young Scot from New Brunswick who filled in as a part-time clerk. McNeil, still shaken from the shock of his discovery, told of finding the body and said he had not noticed anyone near the store when they drove up in the sleigh.

Inspecting the premises, Dowling saw that the cash drawer was partly open and empty. A question to McKelvie revealed that it should have contained nearly $50. Another clue was found at the rear exit where a small chopping axe, its head and handle covered with blood, lay partly concealed behind a packing box. Nearby, a $1 bill was caught under the door.

Dr. Kennedy finished examining the body. "As close as I can determine," he told Inspector Dowling, "Adam had his back to the assailant. His attacker leaped upon him, probably threw an arm around his head, and slashed his throat with a sharp instrument. There are no signs of a struggle on his body. Whatever the instrument was, it made a slight cut on the left side of the neck, then dug deeply on the right side, severing the windpipe, the major arteries, and leaving a gash about six inches in length. From the position of two cuts on the back of his head, I would suggest that he was struck after he fell to the floor."

"No sign of a struggle," Dowling commented. "Attacked from behind, probably as he opened the cash register. Looks as if he knew his attacker."

"He certainly had no warning," Dr. Kennedy agreed.

Inspector Dowling sent to the police barracks for more men, and then began a closer examination of the crowd for possible witnesses. One, Ed Francis, said that he had been in the store earlier that evening to chat with Adams. While there, he remembered that Jess Williams, a negro cook at the Far West Hotel, had come in to pay a bill. It resulted in a small fuss. Williams had gone behind the counter and personally scratched his name off the list of those who owed money. Adams told him that he should not have come behind the counter and Williams had gone out muttering that when he paid a debt he wanted proof it was paid. He had quite obviously been drinking. Neither Francis nor Adams were upset by the incident.

Fraser, the confectionery store owner, then recalled that while they were waiting for the police to arrive, Williams had come to the store to ask what the excitement was. On being told that Adams was dead, he had simply made a commonplace remark and left, showing no further interest in the affair. Although there was as yet nothing to connect Williams with the brutal murder, the negro was already a prime suspect. Francis, wittingly or unwittingly, had aroused suspicions when he remarked that when Williams went behind the store counter, he had had ample opportunity to see how much money was in the till.

With the arrival of reinforcements from the detachment, Inspector Dowling took prompt action. He cleared the store, re-examined it, but found nothing to add to the meagre bits of information gathered thus far. His conclusion was that an assailant, or assailants, had tricked Adams into opening the cash drawer, attacked him with a sharp instrument and beaten him with the axe before fleeing through the back door — if the evidence of the dollar bill was to be credited.

Since a wave of antagonism was already being stirred up against Williams and men were beginning to mutter about lynch laws, Dowling dispatched Sergeant-Major Blake with a posse of police to find the suspect.

Feelings were now running high in the little frontier community. In his biography, *Forty Years in Canada,* Inspector Sam Steele wrote of the incident:

"The murder caused a great deal of excitement, and when it was reported a large mob of citizens, headed by a very decent but excited individual, came to find out what I was going to do about it, and there were threats of lynching the perpetrator if captured. But I said to him, 'You lads are all tenderfeet, and have visions before you of taking part in a Neck-tie Social. There never has been a lynching in Canada, nor will there be as long as our force has the police duties to perform, so go away like sensible men, and remember that any attempt at lynching will be bad for those who try it!' This settled the matter . . . ."

Blake's posse had no difficulty locating the shack where Jess Williams lived with his common-law wife, Religious, a Sarcee woman, and his Indian brother-in-law and wife. After posting his men, Blake knocked on the door. It was opened by the suspect himself.

"Jess, I want to talk to you about the killing of young Adams."

"Don't know nothing about it, except what I heard down at the store," the negro informed him blandly.

"We want to search your house," Blake informed him, pushing inside.

"I had nothing to do with that," Williams said.

Inside the shack, while Religious and the other Indians watched in apprehensive silence, Blake examined the man's clothing. On a coat he found a splash of still wet blood.

"How did you get this, Jess?" the policeman demanded.

"Oh, that must be from the beef I carried back from the butcher's place," Williams protested. "You can find the meat in a box at the back of the shack."

Blake found the parcel of meat, neatly wrapped but there was no indication that it had leaked blood. "Jess Williams," he said, "I am arresting you on suspicion of the murder of James Adams. I'll have to take you down to the barracks."

Leaving the two men to question the Indians, Blake escorted his prisoner to Calgary barracks. Here additional bloodstains were found on Williams' clothing, and imprinted against the cloth of a pants pocket was the outline of what one officer suggested might be a case of some kind. While this examination was taking place, a constable returned from the shack with a damning piece of evidence. Shortly after the murder, Williams had arrived at the shack and ordered his wife to heat water to wash some blood from his hands.

A strong guard was placed over the suspect that night, and with the breaking of the cold February dawn, police checked for further evidence. Constable McRae discovered a set of footprints leading away from the back door of the store. Following, he quickly located a blood-stained razor and, further on, a blood-smeared razor case. Recalling that the imprint of such a case had been found on the inside of Jess Williams' pocket, the constable carefully wrapped his grim evidence.

The trail led down the back alley, past the offices of the *Calgary Herald,* and towards the Elbow River to the south. Near the butcher's shed on the Cochrane Ranch, McRae found a bloodstained leather glove. From here, the tracks led to a road which had been traversed several times since the previous night, thus obliterating the footprints. Later, however, the glove was identified by Williams' wife as being the same kind worn by him. In addition, the print from his overshoes matched perfectly those found in the snow behind McKelvie's store.

Even though confronted with this additional circumstantial evidence, Jess Williams loudly continued to voice his innocence. He talked quite freely of himself and told how he had been born in Texas in 1841 and moved north to Detroit after the Civil War. From here he drifted to Canada where he worked as a cook for construction crews on the Canadian Pacific Railway, a job which eventually brought him west. After completion of the railway, he worked as a cook on a ranch and in late 1883 came to Calgary. Here, again, he was employed as a cook for two months but for the past two weeks had been out of work.

On the night of the murder Williams admitted he had been drinking but declined to name the man who sold him the liquor. He admitted going to the store and having a mild argument with Adams, but denied killing him. After his visit to McKelvie's Store he went to the butcher's shop, paid a small bill, bought some beef — from which he obtained the tell-tale bloodstains — and heard a commotion at McKelvie's Store. On going there, he learned that Adams had committed suicide, or been murdered. It being no business of his, he said, he had returned home.

At this point, the first break came. Williams admitted that the glove found near the butcher's shop was his. Unknown to him, some ranch-hands on the nearby Cochrane Ranch had discovered the mate to the glove stuffed under some hay on a hayrack. Inside the glove was the stolen money — less than $50 for which Adams had wantonly been slain.

Evidently the killer when fleeing the store had thrust the money into the glove and concealed it in the hay, intending to return for it later. Pure chance had revealed its hiding place.

With great reluctance, Williams admitted that this was the mate to the glove found beside the footprints in the snow, but feebly tried to protest than an unknown stranger had given him the money and told him to hide it. Following this explanation he requested an interview with Inspector Dowling.

He confessed that he had killed Adams then afterward gave an interview with Thomas B. Brayden, who the year before co-founded a newspaper with the impressive name *The Calgary Herald, Mining and Ranche Advocate and General Advertiser*. On February 14, 1884, the paper reported: " 'I have confessed the crime to the Commanding Officer voluntarily, and I may as well tell you. On Friday night I went to McKelvie's store to settle a little bill I owed, and saw deceased and another gentleman present; after paying the account I asked deceased for a pencil which was given me. I went forward and scratched out the account which was recorded on the wall; deceased said I should not have done this; I answered the debt was paid, and I wanted it blotted out.

" 'The other gentleman then went out; deceased and I began wrestling or fooling, and in the fray, Mr. Adams received a slight hurt, and got angry, saying that this must be stopped or there would be a fuss. I said there was no fear of a fuss; seeing a razor on the counter I picked it up and struck at him, not meaning to hurt him, but cut a gash on the left side of his throat.

" 'Seeing I had injured him more than I intended, I thought I would finish him, which I did with the razor; I then went out but seeing no one, I came back, and as the deceased seemed to be suffering, I picked up the axe and struck him with it to put him out of pain; I then went to the drawer and took out the money; went to the bank of the Elbow River and hid it; I then started for home.' "

Feelings were running high in the little frontier town of Calgary, and the police quickly brought Williams before a court. On February 20, trial was held before Judge Macleod of the NWMP and a jury comprised of some of Calgary's leading citizens. Throughout the trial Williams listened impassively to the evidence. At times he smiled, though the effect was marred by a cast in his left eye that gave his face a sinister appearance.

He was well defended by a lawyer named James A. Lougheed but the evidence was overwhelming and the jury found him guilty without leaving the box. Judge Macleod sentenced Williams to hang on March 29, less than two months after he had committed the crime.

"Some weeks later the sentence of the court was carried out," Sam Steele wrote, "the prisoner marching to the scaffold with a jaunty, military step, keeping time with the escort, and on the scaffold he faced the witnesses to the execution, and stated that drink was the cause of the crime. Dr. Kennedy and I were the official witnesses, and I relate these circumstances for the reason that this was the first execution in the North West Territories of any person other than an Indian, and it was carried out in the barrack square of the Mounted Police."

The Murder of Sergeant Wilde

**The tragic sequence of events unfurled when an
Indian nicknamed Charcoal again caught Medicine Pipe
Stem seducing one of his two wives. Charcoal
terminated the affair with a Winchester bullet
through the dusky Lothario's left eye.**

Sergeant Brock Wilde, seated at left, with fellow NWMP officers at Pincher Creek the year before he was murdered.

Sergeant William Brock Wilde of the North-West Mounted Police reined in his great black gelding, Major, and gazed over the mighty panorama of mountain and prairie in southern Alberta. It was October 1896, the tang of autumn in the air. The groves of poplar were a brilliant yellow and to the west fresh snow scintillated on the rugged peaks of the Rockies which rolled down in purple convolutions to the plain, masking the entrance to the Crows Nest Pass 40 km (25 miles) to the west. To the east the reaches of grass-covered prairie heaved like a straw-colored sea, stretching to the Blood and Peigan Indian reserves and far beyond.

Touching his mount with his spurs the Sergeant followed the trail that dipped into a fold in the prairie which all but hid the pioneer settlement of Pincher Creek. As he jogged down the narrow main street between rows of shaggy Indian cayuses tied to hitching-rails, he acknowledged with a wave the raucous greetings of tweed-clad remittance men and long-limbed cow-pokes. Halting before the log-walled barracks, he entered the guardroom and slammed his Stetson on a peg. Then he rolled a cigarette and turned to Constable Murison. "Well, what's new?"

"Circle-C reports another bunch of steers missing," the Constable replied. "They blame old Crow Eagle's Peigans!"

"Crow Eagle!" Wilde expelled a cloud of smoke. "Why in hell," he growled, "did I ever come to this God-forsaken spot to round up rustled stock. If only there was a little excitement to wake things up!"

Little did Wilde realize that a few miles away on the Blood Indian Reserve had already occurred an event that would provide not only the Sergeant but the NWMP with enough excitement to keep them active for many days. A few days before on the reserve six Indian girls had quirted their ponies across the grassland, looking for wood for the tipi fires.

One of them, Troubles Shining, swung her pinto towards the boundary of the Cochrane Ranch, leapt to the ground, mounted a fence and pointed towards a tumbled-down log shed. Next moment she was joined by Singing-On-The-Shore and the other girls. As they reached the shed and peered through the holes between the logs Singing-On-The-Shore saw something that caused her to gasp. Lying outstretched on a pile of hay was the body of young Medicine Pipe Stem, the admired of every girl on the reserve. At first it looked as though he'd been indulging too liberally in the white man's fire-water. But a second glance told the horrified girl that the handsome, six-foot Lothario of the Blood lodges was dead.

Thoroughly frightened, the girls leapt on their horses and rode rapidly away, all promising to be silent. But gradually the moccasin-telegraph carried the news from tipi to tipi and hut to hut until Medicine Pipe Stem's death was known throughout the sprawling reserve.

On the evening of October 12, 1896 — two days after the discovery of the dead Indian's body — Farm Instructor McNeill lighted the coal-oil lamp in his office at the Blood Indian Agency and stepped over to the window to draw the blind. From out of the darkness blossomed a rose of flame, accompanied by the spiteful crack of a rifle and tinkling of broken glass. A flowerpot on the window-sill exploded, scattering soil in all directions. Blinded by the spraying dirt, McNeill groaned and sank to the floor, clutching his left side from which oozed ominous scarlet stains.

Within a few minutes Indian Agent Robert Wilson was administering to the wounded man what rudimentary knowledge he possessed. "For God's sake, McNeill," he stammered. "What happened?"

"Damned if I know," groaned McNeill, his face contorted with pain, "I just can't figure it out. I was standing at the window when all hell suddenly broke loose."

A check showed that the bullet had been fired from out on the prairie. After striking the flowerpot and seriously wounding McNeill, it passed through the rear wall of the office, struck a window-casing and fell to the floor. "A Winchester .44." Wilson examined it closely. "Could have come from any one of a hundred rifles around here. If it hadn't been for that flowerpot deflecting the bullet, Mac, you'd be a dead man now!"

Hardly had McNeill been made comfortable and the flow of blood stopped when trader Joe Makin galloped up. "Medicine Pipe Stem's dead!" he said excitedly. "I've just found his body. My wife heard about some women finding an Indian lying on a pile of hay in a shack near the Cochrane Ranch. Figurin' it was some young buck sleeping off a load of hootch, I moseyed over and found him. Pipe was stretched out with his head on a beaded vest, dead as a doornail."

"Thanks!" Wilson wearily mopped his brow. Confused, and not a little alarmed, he promptly got in touch with Superintendent Sam Steele, Officer Commanding, "D" Division of the North-West Mounted Police at Fort Macleod.

A few hours later Constable Murison and Police Sergeant W.D. Anderson, guided by Indian police scout Falling Pine, arrived at the deserted cattle shed. Examination of the body disclosed no sign of violence, although there was dried blood on his shirt and blood had run from his nose and mouth. They removed the body to the police detachment at Big Bend. At an autopsy a few days later Dr. Haultain discovered that Medicine Pipe Stem had been murdered. The bullet had entered his left eye and killed him instantly.

"It looks to me," Superintendent Sam Steele later summarized to Inspector A.M. Jarvis, "as though there's some woman behind this business. Right now we're sitting on a powder-keg with all these disgruntled Indians penned on reserves. We've simply got to get the murderer just as quickly as we can and show these Indians we're standing for no nonsense." He heaved his thickset figure from the chair. "I'm leaving this whole investigation to you. Check up with Indian Agent Wilson and see what's behind the attempt to kill McNeill."

Convinced there was some connection between the killing of the young Blackfoot, Medicine Pipe Stem, and the attempt on McNeill's life, Jarvis proceeded methodically to comb the reserve and grill bucks and squaws. The dead man, he learned, had been missed by relatives for quite a few days though none knew anything of his movements. Everywhere Jarvis was met by tight lips and granite faces, while his approach was usually the signal for broad-backed squaws to peg down tipi flaps or barricade cabin doors.

Frustrated, and realizing that delay in arresting the killer would have a serious effect on the Force's prestige, Jarvis turned to the Blood Indian police scouts. Rounding up Chief Scout Green Grass, Many Tail Feathers and Falling Pine, he turned them loose with liberal directions to listen to lodgefire gossip and report any clues they might stumble across.

Then suddenly the stalemate was broken. From a halfbreed girl, Ann Healy, the Inspector learned that a couple of weeks before, Bad Young Man — more popularly known as Charcoal, a quick-tempered and athletic young brave — had returned unexpectedly to his tipi to find his latest wife, Pretty Wolverine, in a clump of poplars engaged in amorous dalliance with Medicine Pipe Stem. Though chased away from the vicinity, the insistent young man, with the connivance of Pretty Wolverine, had continued his illicit lovemaking when Charcoal was busy haying for the NWMP. He was caught again and threatened with vengeance. On the day of Medicine Pipe Stem's disappearance, the halfbreed girl related, Charcoal had ordered his wife to help tramp down hay in the rack. Pretty Wolverine had other ideas. "I'm sick in the head," she told him, "I can't go."

Charcoal had forced the girl to accompany him, while keeping an alert eye on his rival. Wielding a scythe in the shadow of a willow clump, he watched Medicine Pipe Stem manoeuvre towards the deep grass and suddenly disappear. About the same time Pretty Wolverine disappeared. Worming stealthily through the buffalo grass, Charcoal spotted the horses of the pair grazing nearby. He trailed Medicine Pipe to the cattle-shed and a few moments later was peering through a crack in the logs. Within, as he'd expected, he saw his young wife lying on her back, legs spread, locked in amorous tryst with Medicine Pipe Stem. Beside himself with anger, Charcoal had dragged her back to his lodge. And nobody had seen Medicine Pipe Stem since. Such was the gist of the girl's story.

Exhultant though he was at this lead, Jarvis was still perplexed as his horse trotted towards the Agency. What possible connection could there be between Charcoal's probable slaying of the Indian who'd played fast and loose with one of his wives and the attempted murder of McNeill? With his mind in turmoil he reached the Blood Agency to find Falling Pine awaiting him.

The Indian scout expelled a puff of acrid *kinni-kinnick* smoke and nodded gravely. "Charcoal him heap crazy," he said, his eyes fixed on Jarvis. Then in the sonorous Blackfoot tongue he told the first chapter in a drama that sent the Mounted Police on one of the most gruelling chases in their history and brought tragedy and terror to the rolling prairies.

Shortly after his talk with the Inspector, Falling Pine had ridden back to his tipi. After dark he'd been awakened by the snorting of horses. A moment later a shadowy figure slunk into his lodge carrying a gun. Stirring up the embers of the lodge fire so that they threw a flickering light, he recognized Charcoal. "I'm in trouble," Charcoal told him as he hungrily devoured the antelope meat the squaws set before him. "I've killed that dog, Medicine Pipe Stem. Now I'm going to leave the reserve and hunt a living in the mountains . . . and I'll shoot any red-coated *Shimaganis* dog who tries to follow me!"

"The *Shimaganis* have already found the body of Medicine Pipe Stem," Falling Pine informed him. "They think," he added craftily, "that some white man killed him."

As Charcoal continued to talk Falling Pine was thinking. True, Charcoal was an Indian like himself. But he'd committed murder — he was a dangerous man. And Falling Pine knew enough of his people to realize that when one got desperate he often went beserk, killing for the sake of killing, sparing neither friend nor foe. While he was deliberating whether or not to "turn policeman" and capture the killer, Charcoal suddenly leaped to his feet, dived outside and disappeared.

The cause of the tragedy, Pretty Wolverine Woman, in 1910 with her sixth husband, Bob Riding Black Horses. She outlived all others involved, dying in 1946 at eighty-one. At left is the Lothario, Medicine Pipe Stem, his official Indian name Medicine Pipe Man Returning With a Crane War Whoop.

Falling Pine, still imbued with the idea of effecting Charcoal's capture, followed his trail at dawn and overtook him at sunset. Charcoal had fled with his two wives, his mother-in-law, his daughter, two step-sons, tipi and supplies. They were camped in Bull Horn Coulee. Quietly Falling Pine had advised the Indian to stay on the reserve, in which the wives of the fugitive fully concurred. Finally, Charcoal ordered them to strike camp and followed Falling Pine back to his tipi.

But something seemed to arouse the killer's suspicion. "You're trying to fool me," he suddenly said, reining in his mount and preparing to head back to the coulee. Changing his mind he finally entered the scout's tipi and settled for the night. Shamming sleep, he must have watched as Falling Pine slipped stealthily from under his buffalo robe, wormed under the tipi cover and hurried over to Big Snake's lodge to enlist his aid in tying up the murderer. When he returned with Big Snake, Charcoal, horses, baggage and hostages had disappeared.

Inspector Jarvis and Indian Agent Wilson listened with mixed feelings to the scout's story. The Agent was astonished, since he had good reason to believe that Medicine Pipe's avowed enemy, Eagle Moccasin, was the culprit.

Jarvis studied the scout. No longer was there any question as to the identity of the killer, but there still remained the perplexing question of the attempt on McNeill's life. "Is that all that Charcoal told you? Did he say anything about McNeill?"

"Ho!" The Blackfoot lifted a hand to his braided locks. "I meant to tell you. Charcoal said that after he'd killed his wife's lover he decided to get rid of all his enemies who were trying to keep the Indians penned up like cattle in a corral, so he tried to shoot the Indian Agent. When he couldn't get you," his eyes swung to the amazed Robert Wilson, "he decided to shoot McNeill instead. Now, he says he's going to shoot Chief Red Crow because he's too friendly with the whites!"

Jarvis leapt to his feet, certain now that his worries were about over. Charcoal was burdened with six people, food and tipi. There would be no problem catching him and asserting the prestige of the Mounted Police. A hurried message to Superintendent Steele at Fort Macleod galvanized the Force into action. Promptly Steele threw a cordon of scarlet-coated riders along the line of Charcoal's flight and across the base of the Porcupine Hills. While Jarvis, guided by Blood Indian scouts, scoured the valleys in the direction in which the fugitive was heading, another posse rode out of Fort Macleod to prevent him escaping eastward. Still another galloped out of Lees Creek to the southeast to prevent possible escape into the draws and coulees of the Rockies. A final patrol, headed by six-foot-two Sergeant Wilde, barred the way through the rock-walled Crow's Nest Pass and the canyons leading across the British Columbia border.

But the astute Charcoal seemed suddenly to have vanished. For six days the dragnet of red-coated riders, now muffled against the cold in otter-skin caps, short buffalo coats and moccasins, combed prairie, forest and foothills in vain. Finally, scout Many Tail Feathers brought word that the fugitive had crossed the International Boundary to seek sanctuary in the wooded base of Chief Mountain in Glacier National Park.

A portrait of Charcoal taken by famous Western photographer Steele a few days before his execution in March 1897. Clothes were provided by the photographer, the large hat covering Charcoal's handcuffs. By then he was dying rapidly of tuberculosis.

Of the episode, Superintendent Sam Steele wrote in his book, *My Forty Years in Canada:*
"He knew, no doubt, that he would eventually be captured, but was determined to leave a name which would not soon be forgotten, and in this he certainly succeeded. His craft and endurance were remarkable, and excited such admiration that, had he not killed Sergeant Wilde, he would not have been likely to suffer the death penalty, proof having been produced at the trial that he had so much justification in killing Medicine Pipe Stem that no doubt the jury would have returned a verdict of manslaughter only."

Despite Many Tail Feathers insistence, Jarvis divided his party and continued to search, convinced that Charcoal had not crossed the U.S. border. Then he learned that an Indian resembling the wanted man attempted to steal an overcoat from a settler's wagon while he was chopping wood.

Joining forces again that night, Jarvis' posses made a fireless camp in the foothills lest the smoke warn the fugitive and awaited daylight in chilled impatience. As the exploratory rays of dawn tinged the jagged crests of the Rockies with scarlet and gold, the Indian scouts removed their blanket coats and everything that might scrape against the brush and betray their presence. Then police and scouts moved slowly and silently from tree to tree and willow clump to willow clump. For 8 kilometers (5 miles) the posses crept onward. Suddenly from the Blood scouts on the left came a signal. Peering through the screen of interlacing willows the searchers saw, rising from the center of the valley and only half revealed in a gossamer wreath of mist, a single smoke-stained tipi. They had found the fleeing Charcoal.

Squirming like snakes down the bush-strewn valley, Mounties, scouts and halfbreed flankers were within 45 meters (50 yards) when a young rookie stepped on a dried twig. As it snapped beneath his foot the sound echoed in the still morning air like a gunshot. Next second Charcoal jack-knifed through the tipi door, casting swift glances about him. In defiance of orders an Indian tracker raised his gun and fired. Charcoal slipped behind the tipi, dived into the bush and sent a defiant shot whining towards the encircling police. Inspector Jarvis was fortunate. The bullet whipped his hat from his head and creased his scalp.

With Indian scouts pouring volley after volley into the scrub the police rushed the tent to find Charcoal's mother-in-law, daughter and a step-son. Their release, plus the capture of provisions, tipi and horses was serious for the fugitive. The odds against the elusive Charcoal were mounting. Again a wide circle of armed men was thrown around him. With the outlaw ready to kill at the slightest pretext, the chase had now resolved into a deadly drama, with death the certain penalty for careless-ness. Again the posse proceeded to close in on the spot where the Indian was thought to be cornered. A rustle echoed through the underbrush. "There he is!" someone shouted.

"For God's sake men — don't shoot!" Jarvis' affrighted voice rang out. "Those are our men."

The left wing had met the right over the ground where Charcoal was supposed to be lurking. The runaway Indian had bored a hole through the human dragnet, his two wives and a step-son unwilling accomplices.

Big Face, a Peigan scout, suddenly galloped up on a sweat-lathered horse. "Charcoal," he yelled, "him steal'um all Mounted Police horses. Him tak'um from Hollowell Ranch."

This news was incredibly embarrassing. Not only had Charcoal slipped, like a specter, through the cordon, he had replenished his lost horses at the expense of the Mounted Police, leaving them dismounted.

Prematurely, Jarvis had sent word by scout to the nearest telegraph office notifying Superintendent Steele at Fort Macleod that he had the desperado surrounded. By this time Commissioner Herchmer at Regina, and all neighboring detachments, would be convinced the chase was over. And now this humiliating letdown.

To Sergeant Wilde at Pincher Creek the first report of the pursuit had brought a desire to be in at the kill. But hardly had he led his posse into the foothills ere a scout brought word of Charcoal's capture. He was disgustedly stabling his horse, Major, when Peigan Joe quirted his sweating pony to the police corral. "Me see Charcoal," the Indian told the astonished Sergeant. "I'm just leave white man's ranch on the creek, four miles north. Charcoal, him come, shake knife in woman's face and steal'um grub."

Rounding up his posse, Wilde thundered in the wake of the scout. At the ranch he found the woman and her children in a state of terror. Picking up the outlaw's trail they pushed over buttes and coulees of the Porcupine Hills, swung back to the Peigan Reserve and discovered the stolen Mounted Police horses in the last stages of exhaustion. Stealing fresh horses from the Peigans, Charcoal had headed back to the hills.

For the ensuing ten days Mounted Police and Indian scouts, bucking cold and blinding blizzards, combed prairies, foothills and coulees. Jarvis realized that unless the Indian was rounded up smartly, the prestige of the Mounted Police with the tribesmen would receive an irreparable blow that could bring serious consequences. Already at Macleod and Pincher Creek, the whites reported a growing insolence among the young bucks that augured ill, especially for the settlers in their scattered homesteads and ranches. In addition, newspapers across the country were increasingly critical over the fact that over 100 policemen, Indians and others were unable to catch one man — still burdened with two women and one youth, and without shelter or supplies.

Shaken by criticism, the Force was aroused to unsparing effort. From Commissioner Herchmer at Regina came brusque orders to spare neither cost nor effort to bring the renegade Indian to justice. Though patrols scoured every possible hiding place, frostbitten ears and feet adding to their general misery, Charcoal continued to evade them with a facility that aroused a grudging admiration.

Meanwhile, rumor crowded rumor. Charcoal was reported here, there and everywhere from places hundreds of kilometers apart. Frightened ranchers' wives were seeing him in every bush and shadow. But Sam Steele remained adamant in his belief that Charcoal was still somewhere in the Porcupine Hills.

As though to deliberately challenge the Force, Charcoal appeared on the night of November 2 at the Mounted Police detachment at Cardston on the southwest border of the reserve. He appropriated some of Inspector Davidson's equipment and shot the lantern out of Sergeant W. Armer's hand when he went to investigate. Like Inspector Jarvis, the Sergeant was extremely fortunate. The bullet — as footprints in the snow later indicated — had been fired from eleven paces. It passed between Armer's arm and body, causing a slight wound on his left side. Three inches to the left and the bullet would have struck Armer's heart.

Afterwards Charcoal headed north but an Indian named Coming

Superintendent Sam Steele was in charge of the manhunt. Charcoal's greatest foes were the Indian scouts of his own tribe. Shown below are, from left, Calf Tail, Black Eagle, Big Rib, Many White Horses, Tail Feathers, Many Mules and Meat Mouth. Of them, Steele noted: "Their tracking and picking up the trail were all that could be desired, in many cases marvellous, for it must be remembered that there were thousands of horses roaming over the district . . . ."

Deer surprised him on the reserve stealing more horses. He escaped Coming Deer's hastily fired rifle bullets then later pulled up in front of a house occupied by Farm Instructor Colonel William Fox. Charcoal saw Fox silhouetted against the blind and trained his rifle on him. Now it was Fox who was favored by fortune. A noise distracted Charcoal and with a war-whoop he galloped into the blackness, rifle unfired.

Emboldened by these near successes at killing a white man he returned again to the Peigan Reserve, leaving his step-son on a river bank. With remarkable courage he entered a tipi where a group of young bucks were gambling. He then noticed a Kootenay Indian watching him through narrowed eye-lids. Charcoal raised his rifle, deciding to terminate the visitor's curiosity. The Kootenay Indian was also fortunate. Charcoal suddenly realized that retaliation might be visited on his step-son and dropped the muzzle. Then he again disappeared into the night. But when he reached the river bank, his step-son was gone.

Later it was learned that the boy had heard a rifle shot and in fear ran away. He later found a cabin belonging to a Peigan Indian and stayed the night. Next morning he was taken to the reserve. Turned over to the policemen, he finally agreed to lead them to his father's camp. But Charcoal was too crafty. From a hilltop he chuckled as he watched his son lead the policemen to his abandoned camp.

But the pace was telling. A couple of days later Charcoal's squaws appeared on the Blood Reserve. They had escaped, even though Charcoal always tied them up when he left camp. This time he merely bound them hand and foot instead of to trees, and left them lying on opposite sides of an improvised tipi floor. Before leaving he told Pretty Wolverine that she'd made too much trouble — that he planned to kill her when he returned. Afterwards the two women succeeded in rolling towards each other and Sleeping Woman managed to loosen Pretty Wolverine's wrists with her sharp teeth. Badly crippled, their moccasins torn to shreds with the rough walking, they were found by scout Rides At Dawn who turned them over to the Mounted Police. Charcoal now faced his enemies alone.

A few nights later, Jack Spear, in his cabin near the Peigan Agency, was aroused by a cautious knock on the door. "Whose house is this?" someone demanded.

Indians gambling within, recognized Charcoal's voice and fearful of his ever-ready bullets, sat frozen. As the demand was repeated in threatening tones each dived to the nearest safety, a hefty squaw vainly attempted to squeeze her 300 pounds through the doors of a small sideboard. "Where does Running Crow live?" rasped the voice from the darkness.

"At the next house," answered a frightened brave.

Riding to Running Crow's cabin, Charcoal remained taut in the saddle. "Bring me food, brothers," he requested. "I'm hungry."

"Come in and we'll give it to you." Running Crow covered the door with his Winchester while his squaws stationed themselves on either side of the door with upraised axes.

But Charcoal's intuitive sense again warned him. Spurring his mount he took the fence at a bound with Constable Hatfield and a party of

Indian scouts close on his heels. Thundering through the night they lost the snowed-in trail, pulled into Pincher Creek at dawn and notified Sergeant Wilde.

Mounting his big black gelding, Major, the Sergeant gathered a posse of Indian scouts and ranchers and spurred through the spinning flakes, headed for Dry Forks to cut off the fugitive's escape to the B.C. border. They were not only successful, they surprised the outlaw calmly kindling a fire in a gully to snatch a hasty meal. With a defiant whoop the trail-worn Charcoal leaped on his mount and galloped off.

"Come back, my friend," Many Chiefs of the Peigans yelled after him, "and nobody will harm you."

For a second the fugitive reined in his horse, undecided. Then scout Coming Deer hove in sight, shrieking threats. Charcoal laid the quirt across his horse's flanks and was swallowed up in a spume of driving snow.

Sergeant Wilde's funeral, his horse, Major, behind the gun carriage. Major was later sent to England and presented to Wilde's former regiment by Prime Minister Sir Wilfrid Laurier. Of Wilde, Steele noted: "He was one of the finest men who had served in the Mounted Police, faithful, true and brave, useful in every capacity. The citizens of Pincher Creek erected a monument to his memory. Poor Wilde had two large and faithful hounds always on guard where he was, and when the pall-bearers entered his room at Pincher Creek to remove his remains, one of the animals would let no one approach and had to be shot."

Riding the swiftest mount on the Peigan Reserve, Jack Spear was quickly on his tail. But the look of hate that Charcoal shot over his shoulder caused him to hesitate. Twice Jack galloped his big grey head to head with Charcoal's horse but each time a significant movement of the blanket-enshrouded gun across Charcoal's thighs caused him to falter and drop behind.

"Let's change horses," police interpreter Hatfield and Many Tail Feathers urged him. But Spear refused to make the exchange that would have brought Charcoal's flight to a swift end.

Careening through the snow whipped by a bitter northwest wind, Sergeant Wilde sighted the fleeing Indian ahead. He put spurs to Major, sending the magnificent animal plunging through the three-foot snowdrifts and rapidly shortening the distance. With Major's legs hitting the frozen earth like pistons the Sergeant swept on, swiftly overtaking the blanketed Indian. Forgetful of Sam Steele's orders to take no chances,

ignoring the holstered revolver with which he could easily have tumbled his quarry to earth, Wilde leaned forward to yank the Indian from the saddle.

"Stop!" he shouted.

"Get away!" Charcoal snarled a warning.

As Wilde was about to grab his quarry a muffled report came from the blanket. For a second the tall form of the Mountie recoiled, then swayed in the saddle and hurtled to the snow.

Uttering a victorious whoop, Charcoal swung his mount and leaped from the saddle. He leaned over the wounded officer and, placing the muzzle of his Winchester against his forehead, pulled the trigger. In an instant he was astride the dead man's horse, then disappeared like a ghost in the driving snow.

Aroused by the cold-blooded killing of his friend, scout Many Tail Feathers mounted Charcoal's abandoned horse and spurred through the billowing drifts to exact vengeance. Through the bitter night the chase continued, the scout herding the fugitive towards the reserve. Then thickening snow wiped out all sign of the trail. Next day Many Tail Feathers, worn, weary and almost frozen, staggered into the barracks. For 150 km (90 miles), without food or rest, he'd ridden over blizzard-lashed hills, buttes and prairie only to lose the trail at last.

Meanwhile, Wilde's comrades had carried his body to the nearby cabin of John Didapore. Next day it was conveyed by packhorse through a crowd of tight-lipped Pincher Creek residents to the barracks.

Anger and humiliation was felt by every member of the Force. With greater vigor Superintendent Steele pressed operations. Accompanied by the devoted Many Tail Feathers, who'd hardly stopped to rest, Inspector Sanders spurred out of Pincher Creek at the head of fifteen friends of the dead Mountie, all bent on vengeance. Once Charcoal was sighted on a mountainside, covering his pursuers with a rifle. But the Indian scout who spotted him prudently held back the information until the party was out of range.

With newspapers thundering denunciations at the Force's inability to cope with one lone Indian, while disregarding the difficulties which the men faced, Jarvis decided on a new line of action. Behind the bars of the Fort Macleod guardhouse was Charcoal's brother, Left Hand, jailed on a minor charge to prevent him from assisting the outlaw. "Charcoal is your brother," the Inspector said, closely watching Left Hand, "but no man calls a murderer a kin. Charcoal's hand is red with blood. It's raised against your people and mine. He must be captured without spilling more blood. Charcoal is hungry and tired with no place to go. Sooner or later he'll be forced by cold and hunger to come to his relatives for aid. If you promise to help us we will let you return to your cabin."

For a long time the Indian's black eyes searched the Inspector's face. Finally he nodded.

Not completely trusting Left Hand, the Inspector stationed three constables and Indian scouts to keep watch on the cabin. On the night of November 12 the expected knock sounded on the door of Left Hand's cabin. Casting a sidelong glance at his brother, Bear's Back Bone, also released from jail on similar terms, he called through the door: *"Owenen? — Who is it?"*

"Paka-Pa-Nee-Cape — Bad Young Man — Charcoal," came the cautious answer.

In the darkness Left Hand made out a horse and beside it a dim shape. Gaunt and emaciated, Charcoal entered on moccasined feet, unaware that White Top Knot, one of those delegated to watch the place, had moved stealthily to a clump of willows.

Again some instinct seemed to warn the fugitive that all was not well. Furtively he accepted the pipe handed him by Bear's Back Bone and exhaled the fumes of *kinni-kinnick*. His eyes ever alert, he hungrily devoured the dried meat placed before him, then, warned by a fleeting exchange of glances between his brothers, he made for the door. As he reached for his horse's bridle Left Hand suddenly whipped the Winchester from his hand, encircled him with sinewy arms and yelled for help. From the willows catapulted White Top Knot, landing like a projectile on the outlaw.

As Charcoal was hauled inside, too worn and exhausted to oppose these unexpected enemies, a blanket, deftly tossed by an enormous squaw, descended over his head and shoulders. Bound hand and foot with rawhide lashings, he squatted moodily on the floor. Dawn was breaking when his captors noted an ominous trickle of scarlet oozing down his hands. In a last desperate attempt to outwit his enemies he had stabbed his wrists with an awl.

His wounds bandaged, Charcoal was turned over to the Mounted Police and lodged in the guardhouse at Fort Macleod. To far-flung ranches and prairie homesteads, held in terror, word of the capture brought intense relief. The feeling was shared by the Mounted Police.

Tried before a mixed jury of ranchers, traders and citizens at Fort Macleod, Charcoal heard with impassive countenance his sentence of death by hanging. It was a death that to the Indian mind forever excluded his spirit from the sacred Sandhills. Three months later he ascended the scaffold in the horse corral without a tremor but was so weak that he was hanged sitting in a chair. He died while singing the Indian death song.

For his part in bringing about Charcoal's capture, Left Hand was awarded a chieftainship by the Government. But the Indians refused to recognize this honor. Considering his actions treacherous and unbrotherly, they adopted a hostile attitude towards him. When leading chiefs of the Blood Tribe gathered to pay their last respects to Charcoal, a tall majestic Blackfoot, a childhood friend of the dead man, accosted Left Hand. He hurled at him a torrent of epithets and severely lashed him with his quirt.

On November 9, 1946, Mrs. Black Plume, the former Pretty Wolverine, passed away. For fifty years after Charcoal's death, haughty and unapproachable, she had lived on the Blood Reserve, holding sacred one secret of her chequered life. But on her death-bed she confessed that, disturbed by the sound of Charcoal pushing the muzzle of his gun between the logs of the cattle-shed, Medicine Pipe Stem had paused in his amorous dalliance and looked around. He was shot through the eye while still locked in her embrace.

Ernest Cashel — American Desperado

To hide the evidence Cashel dumped the body of the murdered homesteader into the Red Deer River. North-West Mounted Police Constables Pennycuik and Rogers, however, didn't let the killing go unavenged.

Constable Alick Pennycuik

The Cashels of Buffalo, Wyoming, were known as a mean family. Cashel senior had disappeared shortly after the birth of a third child and left his wife to rear her brood as best she could. The eldest boy was John, who by the time he was eighteen had been involved in several minor scrapes with

the law. His young brother, Ernest, followed closely his brother's example. The third child, a daughter, was purported to have been as callous and hardened as the men. As soon as Ernest was able to fend for himself, Mrs. Cashel abandoned her unruly offspring and moved to Ponoka, Alberta, where she worked as a cook in a lumber camp.

Early in 1901, Ernest Cashel received a year's sentence in the U.S. for larceny. Towards the end of the summer, however, he managed to escape from the prison in Buffalo, Wyoming, and nothing was heard from him until October when he was re-arrested in Kansas. Sheriff Kennedy of Buffalo left for Kansas on October 5, but before he could reach his destination, young Cashel had broken jail and was at large again.

Cashel turned up at his mother's home in Ponoka and shortly after obtained a job on John Phelan's Ranch near Sheppard. He seemed to invite trouble, however, for scarcely had he arrived in Canada than he cashed a worthless cheque in Calgary which resulted in a warrant for his arrest. On October 13, 1902, he was apprehended at his mother's home.

The following day Cashel was turned over to Chief English of the Calgary City Police, and the pair started by train for Calgary. In a ruse as old as outlawry, Cashel requested permission to visit the washroom. The obliging Chief English waited outside only to discover that his prisoner had escaped through the window of the slow moving train.

A week later, Cashel stole a bay pony from a ranch near Lacombe and rode eastward to the Mount Lake district. Under the name of Bert

The log shack of homesteader Isaac Rufus Belt who befriended Ernest Cashel, above. In return the desperado robbed and murdered Belt and threw his body into the Red Deer River.

Ellsworth, he found shelter with an unsuspecting homesteader named Isaac Rufus Belt.

Some time shortly before November 1, Cashel murdered Belt, dumped his body into the Red Deer River and decamped with Belt's saddle, horse, some clothing, a shot gun and a small sum of money which included a $50 gold certificate.

It was not until November 19 that Belt's brother-in-law discovered the disappearance and notified the Mounted Police. Constable Alick Pennycuik, who had already achieved fame as a detective in the celebrated O'Brien murder case of 1899 in the Yukon, was assigned to the Belt murder case.

On November 1, Cashel traded the saddle, which had the name "I.R. Belt" printed in pencil on the undercoating, a bridle and $10 in cash for a horse and cart at Lacombe, and headed south to the Sarcee Indian Reserve near Calgary. Calling himself Nick Carter, he persuaded some Indian boys to buy ammunition and clothing for him.

After spending Christmas at the reserve, he headed for the mountains. When his horse tired, he went to the home of rancher Glen Healy and borrowed another — ostensibly to catch his own horse which he said had strayed. When the horse was not returned. Healy notified the police.

Since Healy's description fitted the fugitive known as Cashel, police kept a close watch on the Kananaskis area of the mountains, notifying all settlers, miners and businessmen to be on the lookout. When a woman at Kananaskis reported a diamond ring had been taken from her, and a trainman reported the theft of clothing from a caboose at Canmore, the search switched to the mining town of Anthracite, near Banff.

On January 24, 1903, Cashel cashed a cheque at the station in Anthracite but was recognized by Stationmaster W.L. McDonald who notified the police. Cashel was arrested at his boarding house, brought to Calgary and lodged in Mounted Police barracks.

Though Pennycuik was almost certain that Cashel was involved in the disappearance of Isaac Belt, the body was still missing. Nevertheless, on May 14, 1903, Cashel was sentenced to three years in the penitentiary at Stony Mountain, Winnipeg, for the theft of Glen Healy's horse and the diamond ring at Kananaskis. With his man safely in jail Pennycuik pressed forward his investigation.

When the ice broke on the Red Deer River, Constables Pennycuik and Rogers searched some 640 km (400 miles) of river bank in an unsuccessful attempt to find Belt's body. It wasn't until July that John Watson, a farmer some distance below Belt's homestead, found the corpse on the river bank. A .44 caliber bullet extracted from the body matched bullets from the revolver taken from Ernest Cashel at the time of his arrest.

Cashel was charged with murder and committed to stand trial before Judge A.L. Sifton. Though defended by Alberta's foremost criminal lawyer, Paddy Nolan, Cashel had been caught securely in the net of evidence woven by Constable Pennycuik. The jury took only thirty-five minutes to evaluate nine days of trial evidence. On October 25 Judge Sifton sentenced Ernest Cashel to hang in Calgary on December 15, 1903.

In mid-November, John Cashel arrived from Wyoming and began to visit his brother. Less than a month later Cashel escaped, using a pair of revolvers that John had smuggled to him. On December 11, 1903, the Calgary *Daily Herald* reported: "The sole conversation on the streets today is the escape of Cashel. Everybody wants to know the latest developments in the case, but they are forced to go with very little new information.

"At the Police Barracks all is bustle. Descriptions and information are being sent to every part of the country, and particular attention is being paid to all trails, and railways which lead to the United States . . . ."

While John Cashel was quickly arrested on suspicion of supplying the revolvers, Ernest seemed to have vanished. For weeks the newspaper carried stories about the unsuccessful search, including one which, although humorous, could have been tragic.

On December 18, 1903, the paper reported: "An old lady, who is very deaf, went over to the homestead of her son to put the house in proper shape, and prepare a meal for him. The son, who lives alone, was seen by the police quite a way from the house, and when they rode along and saw smoke coming from the chimney, they were sure that somebody was in the house, and that the somebody must be Ernest Cashel. Several times the police called on whoever was inside to come out, but nobody appeared. They fired two or three shots, and still there was no sign of life.

"Finally, one of the police approached the house, opened the door, and found the deaf woman to be the sole occupant. Her deafness had prevented her hearing even the rifle shots."

The NWMP were certain, however, that Cashel was still in the vicinity and continued their search, finally using sixteen officers, sixteen civilians and six soldiers from the Canadian Mounted Rifles. Their diligence proved successful. On January 24 *The Daily Herald* published a special edition with three huge headlines, one modestly titled "GRAPHIC STORY OF THE MOST SENSATIONAL CASE IN THE HISTORY OF CANADA."

"Ernest Cashel is caught at last! He was brought into the N.W.M.P. barracks this afternoon shortly after two o'clock, and is now safely and securely lodged in jail.

"The story of his capture is a most dramatic one. After being at large from the 10th of December to the 24th of January, with all kinds of opportunities to get out of the country, he was finally landed through his own foolhardiness.

"During the last two weeks the police have had several traces of him, but as it was found that he was reading the paper regularly, The Herald at Col. Saunders' request published no news of the chase for several days.

"Over a week ago Cashel went to the ranche of Mr. Coppock's, south of Sheppard, and held up the family with his revolver, taking what cash there was in the house, and examining Mr. Coppock's cheque book. On Thursday last he held up James Wigmore, at whose place he slept. He followed Mr. Wigmore with his guns every time he went out. Two weeks ago he was in Calgary, and during his visit he wrote a letter to Rev. Mr. Litch. The letter was written on a sheet of paper bearing the imprint of a

Ernest Cashel, center, was hanged a week after his recapture.
Calgary's *Daily Herald* published a special edition when he was caught.

The Daily Herald

22ND YEAR. WHOLE NUMBER 5,884. CALGARY ALBERTA, MONDAY JANUARY 25, 1904. PRICE : VE CENTS

Special Edition

Cashel the American Desperado Captured this Afternoon

SURROUNDED BY POSSE AND DRIVEN OUT BY FIR

GRAPHIC STORY OF THE MOST SENSATIONAL CASE THE HISTORY OF CANADA.

Ernest Cashel is caught at last!

He was brought into the N. W. M. P. barracks this afternoon shortly after two o'clock, and is now safely and securely lodged in jail.

The story of his capture is a most dramatic one. After his escape from the 16th of December to the 24th of city hotel. In it he asked Mr. Litch to advise Radcliffe (the hangman) to go home, as he (Cashel) expected to live a while longer. He said he was very comfortable, and had plenty of friends, read the Daily Herald, and knew all that was going on.''

His freedom ended on January 24 when Mounted Police under Inspector Duffus, assisted by a troop from the Canadian Mounted Rifles, closed in on Pitman's Ranch about 11 km (7 miles) east of Calgary. They discovered a haystack containing a blanket and a mattress that had obviously been a hideout, but Cashel was not there. Nearby, a ranch bunkhouse appeared to be empty until a trapdoor was discovered in the floor.

Constable Biggs started to descend but quickly retreated when fired at twice by Cashel. When the convict ignored repeated demands to surrender. Duffus ordered the bunkhouse set on fire. Cashel soon came up, hands above his head. "God, boys, I don't want to be hanged," he said, "and I don't want to kill any of you, but I guess I'll have to give myself up.''

Just over a week later Cashel was dead. On February 2, 1904, the *Daily Herald* reported: "Ernest Cashel was hanged this morning and satisified with his life the demands of justice. He died firm, but with an easy conscience, for shortly before the fatal moment he told the Rev. Mr. Kerby that he was guilty of the murder of Isaac Rufus Belt.

"The whole hanging was quietly done and from the time the condemned man left the guard room until the drop fell two minutes were not consumed.

"When all was ready Radcliffe (the hangman) warned everyone away from the trap and gave the signal to Mr. Kerby to start the Lord's Prayer.

"This the reverend gentleman did. He repeated the words: 'Our Father, which art in Heaven,' and on down in a slow, and distinct voice. When the words 'Lead us not into,' were spoken, Radcliffe let down the trap and Cashel dropped below, a distance of 10 feet.

"After Cashel had been hanging about two minutes, Dr. Rouleau, the N.W.M.P. physician, felt the pulse of the hanging man, and said it was still throbbing, but very faintly.

"Radcliffe said 'Let him hang about 20 minutes,' which was done. At the expiration of this time he was cut down and carried into a tent in the yard.

"The limp body was laid on a stretcher and a block of wood placed under the head. Then the coroner, Dr. Mackid, and his jury filed in and viewed the corpse.

"After the jury had retired, a Herald representative entered the tent as Radcliffe was examining the body and turning it over.

'' 'Is his neck broken?' asked the newspaper man.

'' 'Feel it,' said Radcliffe, as he gripped it in his big hand.

'' 'No thanks,' said The Herald man.

'' 'Well, you asked me if his neck was broken and I ask you to feel it for yourself.'

"The reporter however expressed his willingness to take the hangman's word for it.''

British Columbia's Wild McLean Gang

Allan McLean

Alexander Hare

"Every one of the prisoners knew that Ussher was a constable and the killing of a constable is at all times a heinous offence. It is especially so in this country where the enforcement of the law depends entirely upon the moral effect which the power of an officer of the law has throughout the country to enforce the law's mandates . . . ."

Thus did Mr. Justice Crease address the jury during the trial of Allan, Charles and Archie McLean and Alex Hare at New Westminster, British Columbia, in March 1880. The four had murdered Provincial Police Constable John Ussher in cold blood, wounded two other men and used a shepherd named Kelly for target practice.

The McLeans were the halfbreed sons of Donald McLean, a

Two of the gang were aged seventeen, a third fifteen. They had nevertheless wounded two men, beaten another almost to death, murdered a British Columbia provincial policeman and used an inoffensive shepherd for target practice.

Charlie McLean

Archie McLean

Hudson's Bay Company chief trader at Kamloops who had in 1849 participated in the murder of several Indians and who was himself killed by an Indian in 1863. Allan, twenty-five, was the oldest, a splendid physical specimen with jet black hair and beard. Charles was seventeen. He was tall and muscular with butting brows and, as one report noted, "a glance that was anything but frank and pleasant." Archie was fifteen, the youngest but fairly tall for his age with dark hair and eyes. An older stepbrother, Hector, lived nearby but was in jail at the time of the murders.

Accustomed to a wild frontier life from birth, the McLean boys lived in the saddle. They could ride as soon as they could walk, rope anything still or moving, and were excellent shots with a rifle or pistol. They spoke the French-Indian patois, as well as Indian Chinook and English.

The four outlaws began to attract attention in the fall of 1879 in the Nicola-Okanagan districts of southwestern British Columbia. They had formed a sort of gang which included Alex Hare, the seventeen-year-old son of a rancher named Nick Hare. It was common talk that person, property and livestock were not safe when the McLeans were around.

For instance, one of the McLeans got into a fight with an Indian and bit the man's nose off. He served a few months for this offence but came out with a yearning for vengeance. A Chinese was robbed by the gang and so badly beaten over the head with a gun butt that his life was endangered. These wild actions were accompanied by wilder talk since the McLeans always threatened their victims with fresh violence. Naturally, this lawlessness could not go unchecked.

Scattered throughout the Interior were officers of the B.C. Provincial Police. The detachment areas were vast, the population scattered and communication difficult. The railway had not yet arrived, with stage-coaches and packtrains serving the population. There was a telegraph system, though it suffered from frequent breakdowns. The Provincial constable stationed at Kamloops was John Ussher. He was thirty-five, son of a clergyman and had been married about eighteen months. "Johnny" Ussher, as the townspeople called him, was respected by most members of the community. He was well known to the McLeans, having arrested them for minor offences from time to time.

One day early in December 1879, rancher William Palmer who lived about 55 km (35 miles) from Kamloops rode in to report that his black horse had been stolen. Palmer had seen Charles McLean in possession of the animal at the foot of Long Lake. With him were his brothers, Allan and Archie, and Alex Hare. He told Ussher that he had ridden up to the four men and recognized one of them astride his black horse. As he approached, he heard the ominous click of weapons being cocked.

"Don't shoot," said Palmer, "I'm not after you."

"You hadn't better," said Allan McLean quietly. The boys told Palmer of some trouble they had with a rancher named Moore and spoke of "bringing him to time" and, said Archie, "We'll kill any bastard who comes to arrest us."

"Why did you ride up so fast?" one of the gang asked.

"Oh, I just wanted company," said Palmer lamely, then left.

On the basis of Palmer's statement a warrent was issued for the arrest of the McLeans on a charge of stealing Palmer's horse. Knowing that the boys acted as a gang, Constable Ussher first arrested their stepbrother, Hector. Then the officer swore in Palmer and another man named Shumway as special constables and the trio cantered out of Kamloops on December 7 in search of the gang.

As they took the trail, Ussher told his companions that he didn't think there would be any trouble in arresting the gang. It was just after dark when they reached John McLeod's Ranch. On learning their purpose he agreed to join the police party the next morning at a place called Government Camp. Soon it was apparent that they were on the right track, for at one spot in the freshly fallen snow hoof marks led deeper into

Kamloops in the early 1880s, and typical ranching country in the Kamloops-Nicola Valley area terrorized by the McLean gang.

a thick patch of bush. Suddenly, in a clearing they saw four saddled horses.

"They'll never fire a shot," said Ussher. "Come on, I'll take the lead."

They had ridden but a few paces when beetle-browed Charlie McLean was noticed half hidden behind a tree, his rifle showing. The posse reined up.

"I don't see my black horse," said Palmer.

Charlie McLean gave a sharp whistle. A shot rang out and the bullet cut through Palmer's ice-coated beard. "That was a close one," he said, trying to control his startled horse. But the same ball had hit John McLeod. He dismounted, blood spurting from his cheeks.

Then Allan McLean was sighted taking aim from behind a tree. Palmer, armed with a shotgun, tried to get a shot at him as he dodged behind another tree. Allan fired again.

Ussher's horse, startled by the shooting, plunged and reared. Ussher slipped from the saddle. A less courageous man might have been tempted to take cover, but Ussher knew his duty — he was a brave man. He had a revolver in his saddle holster but he left it there, perhaps thinking that his previous contact with the McLeans had earned their respect. It was a tragic misjudgment.

Ussher called on them to surrender. Then, with a deadly fusilade still going on, walked towards Alex Hare. Hare advanced, hunting knife in one hand, revolver in the other. The constable grasped the young man by the shoulder. They grappled. Hare struck repeatedly with the knife. Down went Ussher, Hare astride him. Again and again Hare used the knife, slashing Ussher in the face.

Allan McLean was heard to shout, "Kill the . . . ."

Fifteen-year-old Archie darted from the shelter of a tree, revolver in hand. Holding it close to Ussher's head, he fired. Ussher lay still.

John McLeod, although hampered by the wound to his face, blasted at the outlaws with his shotgun until he was shot in the leg. As Allan McLean was loading his gun, Palmer rode in and fired at him but missed. Shumway was unarmed and could only take cover. After exchanging about thirty shots, the beaten posse rode back to Kamloops for help.

The townspeople were horrified to hear of the fate of Constable Ussher. Horses, arms and ammunition were hastily collected and a large body of horsemen galloped out of town to catch up with the McLeans. Arriving at the outlaw's camp just after dark, they found the camp fire still burning and the body of Ussher frozen stiff. The outlaws had stripped off his coat, boots and gloves.

In the meantime, the McLeans had ridden up to Tom Trapp's homestead some 11 km (7 miles) distant, Trapp recognized them but naturally had no knowledge of the murder.

"What do you fellows want?" Trapp asked.

Charlie and Archie cocked their weapons and said they wanted firearms and ammunition. Eyeing the weapons, Trapp told them to go into the house and take what they wanted. As Allan McLean and Hare dismounted, Trapp noticed a pair of handcuffs dangling from Allan's hand. He also noticed they were bloodstained. Apprehensively, he studied the others.

"You've got blood on you," he said to one of them.

"Yes, Ussher's blood. We killed him." Charlie brandished a knife and boasted of the murder, threatening to kill anyone who came after him.

The boys were carried away with their exploit. In fact Hare and Allan openly debated whether they would shoot Trapp there and then. But they appeared to have had second thoughts about it and rode away with Trapp yelling after them, "You'd better surrender or leave the country."

South on the wagon trail rode the outlaws. In the evening they stopped at another homestead where a man named Roberts was pig killing. He looked up to see four young horsemen around him and noticed they swung their rifles down. "Good evening," he said civilly. "It's a cold night."

"It sure is," answered Charlie, "and a hell of a lot of colder nights coming."

To which the youngest one added, "and a damn sight hotter times, too."

Allan and Archie dismounted and approached Robert's fire, pulling revolvers as they asked for a man named Johnson. Apparently they had some score they wanted to settle with him.

"He's on his own place," said Roberts.

Then they asked about Canda, a local Indian who was noted for his bravery and who was credited with once tangling with three bears. The gang mentioned this incident and Allan said: "This'll be the last night he'll have to face three bears."

"He'll have to face four boys," Archie added. "I'm only fifteen but you bet your life I'm brave."

They then told Roberts they had killed Constable Ussher. "You're fooling," Roberts replied, unbelievingly.

"You bet we killed him," said Allan.

"Here's the knife that went through him, and here's his blood on it," said Hare.

Archie held up one foot, "Here's his boots."

"And here's his coat and gloves," added Hare.

Roberts was horrified, but the McLeans had not finished. Allan drew his attention to the horses standing nearby, saying, "There's his horse, saddle and canteen." Then he went on to describe how William Palmer had ridden in and tried to shoot him. He pointed to some shot holes in his coat and boastfully hauled Ussher's handcuffs from the saddle bag.

"Here's the handcuffs that Ussher brought to put on me — but he didn't get them on. I'll keep them for Palmer."

"Yes," broke in Charlie, "and we'll give him fifty lashes every day and fifty every night before he goes to bed." At this, Allan and Charlie laughed heartily.

They mentioned two ranchers named Ben and Sam Moore and boasted they were going to "get" them. Sickened by this talk, Roberts remarked, "I don't give a damn what you do. You can kill me if you want to."

"No, we don't want to kill you," Allan replied. "You've a large family."

And with that the boys mounted and rode off. Next day, near Stump Lake, they spied a man named Kelly who worked as a shepherd for a settler. Kelly was sitting on a high rock.

"I'll bet I could bring him down from here," bragged Charlie McLean.

There was one report from his rifle and the unfortunate Kelly slithered down the rock. He was dead. Hare ran forward and took a watch and chain from the body.

On they went, boasting of their exploits to workers at Thomas Scott's Ranch. Further south at William Palmer's Ranch they forced Palmer's wife to hand over firearms and ammunition, threatening to kill anyone who barred their path.

They slept that night at an Indian rancherie at the head of the Nicola River. Seeking sanctuary with the Indians was part of Allan's plan and the reason for collecting all the arms and ammunition they could find. If a posse pursued them the gang would arm the Indians and precipitate an uprising. It would spread like bushfire, and the scattered settlements would have something more important to think about than the immediate capture of the McLeans. In any event, even if only a few Indians joined, the whole Nicola Valley would for the time being be at their mercy as the settlers were widely scattered and lacked arms.

Next morning the gang rode in to an Indian ranch at the foot of

John McLean, above, father of the McLeans. In 1849 he helped murder three Indians but was himself shot dead by the Indians in 1864. The other photo shows rancher John McLeod, wounded at the same time Constable Ussher was murdered.

Douglas Lake. They stabled their horses and stayed that day and night.

In the meantime the posse from Kamloops had increased in numbers. Homesteaders were joining the party to put an end to the lawless band. The telegraph wire to Victoria hummed with the news, and Attorney-General G.A. Walkem conferred with the Superintendent of Police who hastened by schooner to Port Angeles, Washington, to alert U.S. authorities to watch the border crossing at Colville in the Okanagan. B.C. lawmen, however, did not think the McLeans would cross the line for they had fought with American Indians and usually worsted them. On one occasion the gang had ridden into an encampment on the American side and after stealing a number of horses, had taken one of the squaws and shaved her head. This was the ultimate insult, assuring the McLeans a potentially deadly reception from Washington braves if they ventured across the border.

The Kamloops posse, led by Justice of the Peace John Clapperton, had by now learned of the outlaws' whereabouts and converged on the cabin they occupied. They were told that a man named Thomas Richardson had parleyed with the gang through two Indians friendly to them. Richardson told the outlaws that they should surrender.

"Never," they yelled, "death before surrender."

When Clapperton heard this news he decided that no unauthorized person should meet with the outlaws. If the Indians were disposed to be friendly to the besieged boys, a general fight might ensue. Clapperton sent word to Chief Shillitnetza to stop all communication between his people

The cabin in which the McLeans were besieged and surrendered.

and the McLeans. The Chief co-operated fully, telling the whites "to shoot any Indian found going or coming from the McLean cabin."

Clapperton was a shrewd frontiersman — he wanted the killers out of the cabin with the least bloodshed. He knew that they had neither food nor water and must eventually give up or commit suicide. He split the posse into three shifts so that there was a constant watch. "Shillitnetza" was the password.

Morning came with no sign of life from the small cabin, though later in the day Clapperton detected through field glasses signs that thirst was troubling the boys. They had torn up the cabin's floor to reinforce the walls, and through a chink in the logs near the ground could be seen attempting to scrape in a little snow. Rifle bullets from the posse smashing into the logs quickly stopped the attempt. Then they tried poking straws through to suck up any moisture. Apart from this activity, the day passed uneventfully. On December 11, a second party of settlers arrived under the leadership of another J.P. named Edwards.

Then Clapperton asked Chief Shillitnetza if his son, Saliesta, would take a message to the McLeans under cover of a white flag. The Indian boy agreed and Clapperton wrote out the following message:

McLean Bros. and Alex Hare: Will you surrender quietly? If so, send in your arms and I guarantee your personal safety. No surrender, and we burn the house over your heads.
Jn. Clapperton, J.P.

With the Indian messenger paper and pencil were sent for a reply. Saliesta reined in his horse about 90 m (300 ft.) from the cabin and waved his signal of truce. Finally, through a crack in the cabin door a tiny piece of rag fluttered for a moment in the raw December air. The Indian moved to within speaking distance. More minutes passed. He advanced to the door and was handed a paper. Bending low in the saddle, Saliesta galloped back to the watching ranchers.

On the scrap of paper, Clapperton read:

Mr. Clapperton,
Sir:—

The boys say that they will not surrender, and so you can burn the house a thousand times over.
Alexr. J. Hare.

I wish to know what you all have against me. If you have anything, please let me know what it is.
A.H.

Clapperton decided to carry out his threat and burn the cabin. Large bundles of hay were dragged into position and saturated with coal oil, but they were wet and refused to burn. For two hours they tried — two hours fraught with danger for the McLeans kept up a desultory fire all the time. In his report on the siege Clapperton noted: "The bullets shot at the bales passed through with deadly force so that the breastwork was useless."

The leader of the posse decided to try another attempt at parley. A man named John Leimard offered to carry the flag this time. He was told to advance and wave it and if an answering signal was shown, to return for instructions. The signal was given, answered, and a settler said he would carry on the parley. He reported that hunger and thirst were doing their work, that the boys were in bad shape. He returned to the cabin with pencil and paper and the outlaws laboriously wrote:

We will surrender if not ironed and supplied with horses to go to Kamloops.

A message was sent back:

Surrender by coming outside and laying down your arms. We will protect you.

Grim-faced ranchers with cocked rifles expectantly viewed the little log structure. Then the cabin door slowly opened and one by one the outlaws appeared. They discharged their firearms in the air, then threw them on the ground. In this act they betrayed their Indian ancestry. It was common practice when Indians surrendered to fire off unused ammunition.

Tired and drawn, their tongues swollen from thirst, the McLean gang staggered forward, hands aloft. Their six revolvers, five rifles and two shotguns were quickly gathered up, and they were handcuffed and placed in a wagon for Kamloops. In the cabin, searchers found John Kelly's watch and chain.

Thanks to the cool and cautious conduct of the two posse leaders, Clapperton and Edwards, the McLean-Hare gang had been captured with but one casualty. A man whose horse had strayed too near the cabin was shot in the chest when he ran forward to retrieve the animal. Fortunately, it was only a flesh wound.

At Kamloops the four were committed for trial on charges of murder. Hare made a partial confession, and intimated that the gang had expected aid from the Nicola Indians.

The prisoners were taken to New Westminster and locked up on Christmas Day 1879.

At New Westminster a special Assize opened on March 13, 1880, at which the McLeans and Hare faced the bar of justice. Hector McLean, the oldest brother, charged with aiding and abetting, was held in jail to be dealt with later.

Witnesses for the Crown were examined and cross-examined and at the end of five days Mr. Justice Crease charged the jury in a two-hour speech remarkable for its clarity and force. He complimented the settlers of the Kamloops area for their adherence to the principles of British justice, implying that on other soil the McLeans would probably have been lynched.

The jury was out for twenty-two minutes and returned with a verdict of guilty. Justice Crease then sentenced them to death. On hearing the sentence, Hare remarked, "It's a well deserved sentence, your Lordship."

The prisoners shambled out of court, their heavy old-fashioned leg irons held to the waist by a leather thong. When Allan, who was manacled to Archie, passed William Palmer he viciously kicked him in the leg. The constable in charge struck Allan with a cane and Archie lashed out at the constable before being hustled to the cells. They continued to be troublesome prisoners and there were repeated attempts at escape, in addition to bursts of disorderly conduct.

The McLeans did not hesitate to appeal their sentence on the grounds that as no commission had been issued, there was no Assize, and therefore no trial. The Supreme Court of British Columbia agreed with them, and on June 27, 1880, ruled that the prisoners had been illegally tried. They were to remain in custody until discharged by due course of law.

At Kamloops in October Hector McLean was acquitted of the charge of being an accessory before the fact. A month later, Allan, Charles and Archie McLean, with their accomplice, Hare, were once more placed on trial in New Westminster for the murder of Ussher and Kelly.

Again, the jury found them guilty. The second trial had only served to delay their execution. In confinement they became more unruly than ever and had to be chained to the walls of their cells for days at a time. On one occasion Archie threatened the Warden with an iron bucket, on another a knife was found in Allan's blankets. On one routine examination prison officers discovered that his irons were partially filed through with a file suspected to be from another prisoner.

Then one day a halfbreed named John Henry Makai, serving a short sentence on a liquor charge, asked the Warden if he could act as executioner for the McLeans. Puzzled by this odd request, the Warden told Makai that an official executioner would be used. However, he kept Makai under observation and later learned that the McLean gang had made a compact with him. If Makai was appointed executioner he would secretly cut through the execution ropes and when the trap was sprung, the

The jail in New Westminster where the four killers were hanged.

outlaws would drop unharmed — the few uncut threads breaking under the strain. They would then whip out knives and cut their way to freedom. Makai, on release, was to be rewarded with a hundred head of cattle and forty horses, which he would collect from brother Hector in Kamloops.

For the McLeans, however, there would be no escape. On January 28, 1881, the New Westminster *Mainland Guardian* carried the following news item: "A SINISTER DISPLAY — As we passed the gate of our city gaol yesterday morning, we observed the pieces of timber all cut and shaped in readiness to be put together to form the scaffold on which the McLeans and Hare are to suffer death on Monday morning next. It is bad enough that their minds are now dwelling on their approaching end, but to have their ears assailed with the tap, tap, tap of the hammers that nail together the 'fatal gallows tree' is something terrible to endure . . . ."

The hanging went as scheduled on January 31, with the paper carrying the following account: "Monday morning dawned cold, sharp, and clear. At 7:30 quite a group of our leading citizens had gathered within the four walls of the city prison, (including the scaffold contractors) Messrs. Fry & Calback . . . .

"The condemned men were early attended by their spiritual advisors, Revd. Father Horris and two other priests. After partaking of a light breakfast, devotions were resumed, and the utmost penitence and contribution was displayed by the four culprits. A little before 8 a.m., the executioner proceeded to pinion them by means of stout leather straps: the hands were fastened in front, and a strap passing above the elbows behind. Shortly after, the procession was formed in the following manner:— The Executioner in front, Sheriff Morrison and Prison Surgeon Trew, Chief of Police and Warden of the Gaol, Father Horris and Assistant Priests, Allan and Archie, with a Policeman on each side, Charley and Hare, with Constable on each side; they proceeded to the place of execution, where all eyes were fixed on the unfortunate men; as they passed along, they said 'good-bye' to those near them, and mounted the scaffold in pairs. Hare stood at the West end, Charlie and Allan in the center, Hare was the first to speak; he said: 'I forgive every one and thank everyone for their kindness; I am guilty of the crimes laid to my charge, and justly deserve the impending punishment'. Charlie spoke next, in the same strain; his pale ashy lips and unsteady motion, might have arisen from cold or from the strongly betrayed emotions within. Allan hoped all young men would take a warning by his sad position, and faltered words of thanks to all; he asked forgiveness for his crime, and said he was prepared to enter the unseen and unknown world beyond the grave. Archie followed in the same words almost, which were repeated by the Revd. Father to those in front of the gibbet. The Hangman then adjusted the ropes, commencing with Hare; the signal was given by the Sheriff, and in an instant the doomed men fell. Death appeared to have been almost instantaneous; with the exception of Charlie, who showed slight convulsions, they scarely moved a muscle. After hanging the usual time, the bodies were cut down and decently interred. After the drop fell, something like a sigh of relief escaped from the spectators, who felt that innocent blood had been avenged, and the law vindicated."

Alberta's First Stagecoach Holdup

Although holdups were usually the least of the problems endured by stagecoach passengers, they occasionally added an extra element of danger to a trip.

The Calgary-Edmonton Trail was an historic ribbon of road. The missionary McDougalls — father and son — drove the first herd of domestic cattle over it in 1874 from Fort Edmonton to Morley; throughout the early 1870s illegal whiskey traders from Forts Whoop-Up, Slide Out and Stand Off traversed it with their wagon loads of firewater and furs; and the Alberta Field Force of 1885 moved up it on their way to overtake Big Bear and the murderers of Frog Lake settlers during the Riel

A stagecoach surrounded by horse and oxen teams at Lethbridge in 1890.
The inset photo shows the Calgary-Edmonton stagecoach crossing a mudhole in 1888.

Rebellion. Many strange and fascinating conveyances passed over the old trail, including Indian travois, dog teams and Red River carts. Then between 1883 to 1891 were the stagecoaches that connected the fledgling communities of Edmonton and Calgary.

The first stagecoach left Edmonton on August 6, 1883 — one month before the Canadian Pacific Railway reached Calgary. An enterprising old-timer from Edmonton, Donald MacLeod, started the passenger and mail service between the two prairie settlements. Known as one of the old Northwest's hospitable characters, MacLeod had been a Red River settler before travelling the Carlton Trail in 1875 and settling down as a part-time trader-prospector in Edmonton. His house was always open to friend or visitor. Many a discouraged prospector sponged a meal from Donald MacLeod, the only payment demanded was an interesting story or two. He was a man of strong physique and character and respected by all who had contact with him. He was also a shrewd businessman with a firm belief in the destiny of the West.

His stage usually left Edmonton on a Monday morning from the hitching rail in front of Jasper House. The trip took five days — perhaps — with night rests at such stopping places as Peach Hills, Battle River, Red Deer Crossing and Willow Creek. There were also numerous watering

places with picturesque names like Scarletts, Blindman and Bear's Hill. In theory, the stage was to arrive in Calgary on a Friday night but travel was rather unpredictable and it might be hours or even days late. After a weekend layover in Calgary, the stage started back from the Hudson's Bay store at 9 a.m. Monday morning. A round trip normally took two weeks, although veteran stage travellers knew that this schedule was extremely flexible. For this reason a valuable asset for passengers on not only the Edmonton-Calgary route but also others in Western Canada was a reservoir of patience.

For instance in 1883 Archdeacon J.W. Tims came to Alberta from England. He eventually reached Fort Benton in Montana Territory and noted: "At Fort Benton I had to stay six days until the I.G. Baker Express (an open wagon drawn by four mules) was ready to make its bi-monthly trip to (Fort) Macleod."

From Fort Benton to Fort Macleod was just over 200 miles, the trip taking eight days. "There were no bridges crossing the rivers," the Archdeacon noted, "no fences of any kind and no roads, the only trails being those made by the ox-teams."

At Fort Macleod the Archdeacon discovered another aspect of Western travel — accommodation was bare-boned. ". . . we put up at a restaurant kept by a negress who went by the name of Aunty," he wrote. "It was a long building, one storey in height, with a lean-to at the far end which served as kitchen and Aunty's bedroom. The sleepers provided their own blankets, and slept on the floor. About six a.m. Aunty appeared with a broom, poked each sleeper with it, and told them to get up and roll up their bedding. Then, from the far end of the room, she commenced to sweep the floor and expected everyone to be up with blankets rolled by the time she reached them."

The stagecoach drivers were a special breed, tough resourceful men who have justifiably become part of the Western legend. In its November 23, 1886, edition *The Macleod Gazette* carried the following tribute to them:

"There is no occupation in the world that looks more easy and pleasant at times, and there is none which at other times is more difficult or that requires more care, genuine courage and good management. In the summer, the weather is warm and the rivers easily crossed. When the first cold weather comes, the hills are slippery and the rivers mean, and then it is that the stage driver requires all the self possession, nerve and skill that nature may have endowed him with. All the routes going out of Macleod are difficult ones to drive over at such a time. All these routes are fortunate in possessing careful and skilful drivers.

"At the head of the list of Northwest drivers, Frank Pollinger reigns supreme. Frank is known and admired from Winnipeg to the Rocky Mountains, and north as far as Frenchman's Butte, where he took part in that memorable battle. He has driven over nearly all the four- and six-horse stage routes in the Western States, where his reputation is just as high as it is here. Every horse in his team knows him, and a word from him is as good as a club in the average driver's hands. Frank is a deserved favorite, and the average passenger considers himself in good luck if he gets a seat alongside of him — except in cold and stormy weather, when Polly generally has to hold it down alone unless there is a full house.

"All the others are good drivers and good fellows. The stage driver has generally a very keen sense of his duty. He will always do more for his employers and his horses than he will for himself. The last trip in from Benton, the driver got into difficulty in the river at Frank Strong's Crossing. With the thermometer down below zero, he worked in water nearly up to his waist for some two hours. Without getting dry or warm, he came straight through to Macleod, arriving after dark in the evening, and encased in a solid mass of ice. Even then he delivered his mail and would not stir from his seat until he had made every endeavor to report to the collector of customs. It was a long time before he could thaw out his clothes sufficiently to get them off.

"Yes, stage driving looks pretty when everything is favorable, but the man who undertakes it in winter and gets there is none of your ordinary kind of man but is stamped with a superiority which only requires the opportunity to make him a hero. All honor to him! He may be a hard case but his thousand and one virtues and good qualities cover a multitude of faults."

Among the "multitude of faults" mentioned by the paper was that many of the drivers were classed as "hard drinkers." A frequent stage-coach passenger during Alberta's frontier era was J.D. Higinbotham. He established the first drug store in Lethbridge and wrote a most interesting book, *When The West Was Young*. Of one stagecoach trip with Polly Pollinger driving he noted:

"Needless to say at this period, the streams were devoid of bridges, although ferries crossed High River, also the Old Man near Macleod; but all others we were obliged to ford and sometimes swim. The passengers and mail were put on the 'hurricane deck' of the coach, which, having a high and sloping dashboard, was fairly well adapted for amphibious purposes; however, we usually landed on the opposite bank some distance down-stream from where we entered the water. The drivers were artists in their line and seemed to know these quickly-changing fords by instinct. One of them, the famous 'Polly,' made the boast to me that he could drive his coach and four where I 'couldn't trail a whip.' Years later he had sufficient confidence in me to allow me to handle the 'ribbons' for him on a good piece of trail, while he peacefully slept off a race-day spree on top of the mail sacks . . . .

"These men were heavy drinkers, and in those so-called 'prohibition days' took their 'red-eye' straight. In winter, when the trail was obscured by snow, it might easily be rediscovered by the presence of 'dead soldiers' along the route. These were headless — or neckless — bottles, as the drivers scorned the use of corkscrews, or openers, and simply decapitated them upon the sharp steel tires of the coach."

But despite the drivers' fondness for "red-eye" they were able to cope with hazards which included blizzards, sub-zero temperatures, prairie fires, floods and irate passengers. But on August 23, 1886, a new hazard appeared. That day Alberta's first holdup occurred, the stagecoach between Calgary-Edmonton being the victim.

101

The stage, driver Braden in charge, left the Hudson's Bay Company store that morning on time, forded the Bow River and headed for Fort Edmonton. About 24 km (15 miles) north of Calgary, two armed horsemen forced Braden to stop. Both men were masked — one with a piece of the Union Jack flag; the other, a black cloth. Meeting with no resistance the holdup men first cut open the mail sacks. When they found nothing of importance they relieved the startled driver and passenger of their valuables. Braden was then ordered to drive on while the men mounted and rode west towards the Rocky Mountains.

Although the holdup had taken place just after noon and only a short distance from Calgary's police barracks, it was not until 5.30 p.m. that word reached Superintendent Anthrobus of the North-West Mounted Police. Even then the news was relayed by a passenger rather than the stagecoach company's office. The reason was discovered later. Driver Braden, after retrieving the discarded mail sacks, had decided to resume the trip and suggested that since the mails were intact it was up to the passengers to report their own losses.

From the passenger's description of the bandits, the Superintendent was struck by the resemblance between them and two men who had robbed the De Rainbouville brothers at Elbow River, southwest of Calgary, a short time before. Assembling a posse of seventeen police and civilian volunteers, Anthrobus left for the site of the robbery. He found little in the way of evidence except two sets of horseprints leading westwards through the tall grass. The Superintendent led his posse in pursuit.

They had not gone far from the trail before the grass grew shorter and the ground too hard to hold a set of prints. However, as signs indicated that the bandits had stopped at this point, Anthrobus ordered a thorough search. One of the posse soon found a pair of dusty overalls and a piece of flag partly concealed beneath a large boulder. Another, who had done prison guard duty at the barracks, recognized the overalls as those worn by John Young, a man recently released after serving six months for possession of illegal liquor.

Anthrobus suspected that the holdup men would return to Calgary by one of the back trails. He divided his party into three — one group to ride westwards and then circle south; a second to ride eastwards and also circle south; and the third led by Anthrobus to cover both sides of the Calgary-Edmonton Trail. In this way, a strip some 20 km (12 miles) wide was scoured from the site of the robbery to the outskirts of Calgary. Homesteaders, cowboys, Indians and townspeople were questioned along the way but no one had seen the two men. When the three posses re-assembled at midnight, their only lead was a report of two strangers at the cabin of Scott Krenger, a prospector at Shaganappi Point 19 km (12 miles) west of Calgary.

Krenger, usually called "Clinker Scott," was well known at police headquarters. He never seemed to work, but always managed to survive. When the police called he confirmed that he did indeed have two men staying with him but they couldn't have robbed the stage since they had been in his cabin all week. Superintendent Anthrobus dismissed them as immediate suspects, although he kept them in mind.

A search was then undertaken in Calgary for Young, the man whose overalls had been found with the piece of flag. But he had not been seen in his usual haunts since his release from prison.

A few days later a settler searching for a stolen buckboard visited Krenger's cabin. Although Krenger's horse was tied to the corral there was no sign of him. The settler peered through the cabin's grimy window and was astonished to see Krenger on the floor, obviously dead. His assailant — or assailants — had surprised him for his hands were still covered with flour and there was a half-finished pan of biscuit dough on the table. He had been shot in the stomach. The doctor later placed death on August 25, two days after the stagecoach robbery.

The two men seen in Krenger's cabin by the posse on the night of the holdup had disappeared, but when descriptions of them were checked neither one resembled the elusive Mr. Young. Nevertheless, he remained a prime suspect.

Superintendent Anthrobus believed that the three crimes were linked, if not all perpetrated by the same two men. The robbery of the De Rainbouville brothers, the stagecoach holdup, and the murder of "Clinker Scott" seemed to form a pattern. It was possible there had been a quarrel over the division of spoils and that the men murdered Krenger as a result. Alternatively, Scott may have outlived his usefulness to them as a cover.

With this possibility in mind, and realizing that he was dealing with desperate men, Anthrobus intensified his efforts by engaging famous railroad detective J.L. Benoit to work on the case. At his suggestion NWMP Sergeant Spicer from the Maple Creek detachment was made a special investigator.

Disguised as a prospector, Spicer visited mining camps hoping to pick up the trail of the fugitives, believed to have holed up in the mountains. Nobody, however, had noticed any suspicious characters. At the same time, Sergeant A.R. MacDonnell circulated through Calgary in plain-clothes trying to pick up information that might lead to the wanted men. His task was a risky one, for Calgary was the headquarters of assorted cattle thieves, horse runners and outlaws. When weeks passed without a clue, it seemed that the "Union Jack" bandits had vanished.

Suspicion did focus briefly on a William Mitchell, who was arrested and tried for the De Rainbouville brothers robbery but acquitted by a jury. With no further evidence Detective Benoit felt he could no longer be of use, and Sergeants Spicer and MacDonnell were given other assignments. Anthrobus let it be known that the case was closed.

Hoping this ruse would either bring the wanted men out of hiding or start idle tongues wagging, Anthrobus waited a month before assigning an undercover policeman not known to Calgary's criminal element. But while several hints led him to believe the men were hiding in British Columbia, none proved substantial and the undercover man was removed.

On December 15, 1886, the elusive John Young surrendered to the North-West Mounted Police. He came complete with an air-tight alibi and as a result was not charged with any of the offences. Alberta's first — and only — stagecoach holdup therefore proved to be the perfect crime since the case never was solved.

Death Song from the Poplars

A wandering cow with no known owner in 1895 triggered Western Canada's greatest manhunt. By the time the revolvers, rifles and cannon were silenced, seven men had died, three of them North-West Mounted Policemen.

Almighty Voice, left, and North-West Mounted Policemen guarding the bluff, right center, where he was trapped. From 1878 to 1914 the Mounties carried their Winchester rifles in a sling attached to the saddle pommel as shown on the horse at center.

THE RESTLESS ONES

When Almighty Voice was born in 1874, his parents — John Sounding Sky and his wife, Spotted Calf — belonged to a small band of Swampy Cree Indians under the leadership of One Arrow. In turn, One Arrow's band was part of a loose association of Crees under the general guidance of Chief Beardy. They hunted on the plains of what would become the province of Saskatchewan and wintered around Batoche and the small community of Duck Lake on the South Saskatchewan River.

Chief Beardy was a sly, cantankerous old man who delighted in upsetting the dignity of civil servants. Thus, when the majority of Plains Cree gathered to sign Treaty No. 6 at Fort Carlton in August 1876 which would confine them to reserves, Chief Beardy and his associates sent word that they wanted the treaty makers to come to them. After some bickering,

a compromise was reached. On August 28, 1876, Chief Beardy, One Arrow and nine band councillors agreed to the treaty which gave them the privilege of having some of their own land set aside for them.

The reserve to which One Arrow and his small band retired was near Batoche on the eastern side of the South Saskatchewan River. Its rich, sandy loam was ideally suited to mixed farming — an undertaking of which the Indians knew nothing and cared less. The area comprised open prairie and "islands" of poplar trees in the miles of short prairie grass. These islands, laced with dense underbrush, were known locally as "bluffs."

Here John Sounding Sky and Spotted Calf settled with their one son, Almighty Voice. His Cree name was Kisse-manitou-wayo, but he appeared on the agency records as Jean Baptiste.

On the whole, the One Arrow band was not an industrious one and strongly resisted the efforts of the Indian Agent to "civilize" them. By the spring of 1885 the band had shrunk to fewer than 200 because of starvation and disease. Of the survivors, some twenty were able bodied men who constantly left the reservation without permission and created a problem for the handful of North-West Mounted Police stationed at Carlton and Duck Lake.

When the Riel Rebellion erupted in March 1885, One Arrow and all his warriors joined the uprising. After Riel was defeated One Arrow was deprived of his chieftainship and sentenced to three years in the penitentiary. From then on, the band was without a chief or councillors.

In 1888 R.S. McKenzie was appointed Indian Agent to Duck Lake. He was a thorough, kindly man with a keen insight into human behavior. One of his first acts was to appoint an Indian, Sandy Thomas, as his official interpreter. Then he selected big, rough and ready Louis Marion as Farm Instructor.

Marion threatened and cajoled the Crees to build more substantial houses, plant small grain crops, vegetable gardens and hay fields, and to send their school-age children to the Indian Industrial School at Qu'Appelle. Even John Sounding Sky — one of the more restless braves — yielded to his blandishments or fists and engaged successfully in mixed farming.

By 1895, the people of One Arrow's reserve were struggling out of a state of semi-starvation. But the price had been drastic, with under one hundred men, thirty women and fifty-nine children left, many of them suffering disease and malnutrition. Among the remaining men was young Almighty Voice.

At twenty-one, Almighty Voice was tall and slim with a battle scar on his left cheek that ran from mouth to ear. His small hands and feet, his fair complexion and dark wavy hair, made him a great favorite with the ladies. Because of the preponderance of women, Almighty Voice, like several of the braves, unofficially took two or three wives.

He is credited with acquiring his first wife, the daughter of Napaise, when he was eighteen. Then he added Kapahoo's daughter and in the summer of 1895 wooed and won The Rump's daughter. Then his attention shifted some distance to a thirteen-year-old at the Fort a la Corne Reserve.

Louis Marion, who closely watched his charges and promptly reported absentee braves to the NWMP, never worried about Almighty Voice's wanderings. He correctly presumed that the popular young brave was off in quest of romantic adventure. Nevertheless, while most of the other Crees in the Duck Lake agency were becoming more law abiding and industrious, One Arrow's band remained restless and caused difficulties for Marion and the police.

One example occurred on October 19, 1895. That day John Sounding Sky was arrested for illegally acquiring a piece of farm equipment belonging to L. Couture, whose farm adjoined the reservation. Sounding Sky was found guilty of theft and sentenced to six months hard labor.

The next day, while his father was en route to the prison, Almighty Voice arrived from Fort a la Corne with the thirteen-year-old daughter of an Indian named Old Dust. Her brother, Young Dust, accompanied them.

Almighty Voice's parents — Spotted Calf and John Sounding Sky.

Almighty Voice installed his fourth intended bride in his mother's home and began to prepare for the wedding feast. His current wife, daughter of The Rump, returned to her father.

Meanwhile, the fact that food was scarce did not dampen wedding plans. With Young Dust, Almighty Voice visited friends and invited them to a modest wedding feast that night at John Sounding Sky's house. While returning home, the pair came upon a cow that had wandered onto the reserve. Thus began a sequence of events that culminated in one of the most dramatic manhunts in the Canadian West and resulted in the death of seven men.

As part of the farming experiment, Indian Agent McKenzie had purchased a small herd of cows for the One Arrow band which were pastured on the reserve. In addition, one or two farmers whose property adjoined the reservation also owned cattle. Occasionally, one of the animals disappeared. If it was a settler's cow, the matter was treated with firmness, but if an agency cow the matter was considered less serious. Ironically, the cow encountered by Almighty Voice later proved to be neither. It had strayed several miles from its grazing grounds and no one knew its ownership.

Almighty Voice, however, wasn't concerned about who owned it. With a shot from his .45-75 Winchester he solved the problem of feeding his guests. Thanks to the wandering cow, the wedding feast lasted into the night. News that there was plenty of meat spread quickly through the reserve and uninvited guests began to arrive. Among them was Dubling, brother of Almighty Voice's recently discarded wife. Dubling capped his feast by dropping into Marion's home and informing the farm instructor that Almight Voice had killed an agency cow.

The next day Marion advised Sergeant Colebrook at the Batoche NWMP detachment and then checked his herd. None was missing.

The following day, October 22, was treaty payment time at Duck Lake. As Almighty Voice and Young Duck stepped forward to collect their payments, they were taken into custody by Sergeant Colebrook and turned over to Sergeant Harry Keenan who was in charge of the Duck Lake Detachment.

The prison at Duck Lake was a log shack that had been converted into a guard house by the addition of iron bars to the windows. Inside was a single room with a table and chair near the door. The usual procedure was to allow the prisoners to sleep on the floor while the guard slept in his chair. In the event that a dangerous criminal might be incarcerated, several large iron rings had been embedded in the logs for handcuffs or leg shackles.

During the day, Almighty Voice and Young Dust lounged in the yard, and at night were placed inside the log shed and given blankets. Night duty — especially guarding two peaceful prisoners like Almighty Voice and Young Dust — was boring to Constable Thomas Alexander Dickson. He dozed or played cards until his watch ended at 2 a.m. After a glance at his sleeping prisoners, he walked over to the nearby barracks to awaken Constable Andrew O'Kelly. Not considering his prisoners dangerous, Dickson did not lock the door.

O'Kelly arrived at the guard house some five minutes after Dickson's departure. Young Dust was still sleeping soundly but Almighty Voice had simply walked through the unlocked door into the night.

On learning of the escape Sergeant Keenan, surmising that Almighty Voice would head for John Sounding Sky's cabin, notified Sergeant Colin Colebrook at Batoche. Constable Dickson was sent to assist in the re-apprehension of the young Cree.

Although the Mounted Police were treating the affair with routine casualness, Almighty Voice, impelled by some sense of urgency, made his way directly to the river near Batoche Crossing. The weather was cold, and ice had formed along both banks of the South Saskatchewan River. Nevertheless, he swam across and made his way to his father's house.

During the next few days, Sergeant Colebrook and Constable Dickson made several surprise visits to the reservation without catching sight of their escaped prisoner. Colebrook was sure that Almighty Voice was somewhere on the reserve since his young bride had taken ill after the wedding feast. The continued presence of Young Dust was also reassuring. In the meantime, Police Scout Francis Dumont wandered around the reserve, on the alert for news.

One night Dumont learned that Almighty Voice had secured a pony and left the reserve. His informant suggested that he might be headed for

The jail at Duck Lake in Saskatchewan today has been restored. From it Almighty Voice walked into the night — with tragic consequences.

the John Smith Reservation at Fort a la Corne. Dumont rode to Batoche and told Sergeant Colebrook.

The next morning, Colebrook and Dumont left to trail the escapee. Although skiffs of snow had fallen there was not sufficient to warrant using a sleigh so Colebrook rode in a democrat while Dumont walked his pony. A well travelled trail led from the ferry at Batoche to a settlement at Kinistino 48 km (30 miles) to the east. Dumont picked up Almighty Voice's tracks along the trail and followed them for some distance. They indicated that Almighty Voice was walking while his wife rode.

Towards evening they met Police Scout Joe McKay, better known as "Gentleman Joe," one of the picturesque characters of the West. With his fine white beard he resembled Buffalo Bill of Wild West fame and in 1885 had fired the first shot in the Riel Rebellion at Duck Lake. After the rebellion he continued his career as a police scout and was stationed at Prince Albert. He had now been sent to Fort a la Corne to intercept Almighty Voice if he showed up.

Learning from McKay that heavy snow had fallen east of Kinistino, Colebrook exchanged his team and democrat for the scout's horse. Until now the fugitive's trail led southeastward in the direction of the Touchwood Hills. Just before nightfall, however, Colebrook discovered that Almighty Voice had turned north in the direction of his wife's reservation. He decided to camp on the trail and resume pursuit in the morning.

A POLICEMAN DIES

The morning of October 19, 1895, dawned cool and clear. A week had passed since the casual arrest of Almighty Voice and Young Dust at Duck Lake, but beyond the fact that Sergeant Colebrook and Dumont were tired and cold, nothing had altered the routine approach to apprehending the young Indian. But as Colebrook and Dumont rode along the trail that morning they were startled by the near crack of a rifle. Over a slight rise they saw an Indian pony beside the trail. A young Indian girl squatted beside a small fire, while a short distance away a slender young brave emerged from the trees carrying a dead rabbit.

It was Almighty Voice. Each recognized the other instantly. As Colebrook urged his horse forward the young Indian dropped the rabbit and reloaded his Winchester. Colebrook continued to move forward. Then Almighty Voice called a warning in Cree. The officer's knowledge of Cree was slight but Dumont translated that Almighty Voice intended to shoot.

Ignoring the warning, Colebrook slipped his hand into his pocket and brought out his service revolver. Holding it in his lap, he lifted his free hand in a sign of friendship and urged his horse forward.

Almighty Voice raised his Winchester and covered the advancing officer. Up to this point, Almighty Voice had been a law-abiding if impetuous young man whose worst crime had been killing a stray cow and walking from an unattended jail. Once recaptured, his sentence would probably be a few days work on the woodpile. His adversary, Sergeant Colebrook, was a level-headed police officer familiar with serious situations. He obviously was convinced that the young man would not be foolish enough to shoot.

110

Almighty Voice shouted again. Scout Dumont, warned by his tone of voice, urged the policeman to stop. It was too late. Almighty Voice sent a heavy .45 caliber slug into Colebrook's chest. Stunned momentarily from the impact, he fell from his horse, the unfired revolver slipping from his fingers.

Dumont, fearing for his own life, wheeled his horse and spurred back along the trail until a rise in the ground hid him from view. Scarcely had the police scout decamped than Almighty Voice approached the fallen officer and scooped up his revolver. A glance told him that Colebrook was unconscious. After hurried consultation with his young bride, he mounted the officer's horse and rode eastward. The Indian girl stoically retrieved the rabbit her husband had shot and started to cook it over the fire.

The first policeman Dumont encountered as he headed from the murder scene was Constable Charles Tennent, on patrol with scout Timothy Meyers. Dumont then continued towards Batoche, while Tennent and Meyers rode to where Sergeant Colebrook lay dead. The girl was still eating the rabbit.

Tennent dispatched Meyers to a nearby settler named Harper for a wagon. He took the girl into custody and the party returned to Harper's with Colebrook's body.

In the meantime, Scout Dumont had reported the grim details to Corporal McKenzie at Batoche. Telegraph messages were sent to Duck Lake. Every available man from both detachments immediately saddled up and scoured the countryside for the murderer. From Prince Albert came a special detail commanded by Inspector John B. Allen, better known as "Broncho Jack."

Meanwhile, Almighty Voice's wife had been brought to Duck Lake with the body of the slain officer. She made several contradictory statements concerning the tragic affair, but her testimony added little to the account already given by Dumont. A post mortem revealed that the slug had struck Colebrook's collar bone and deflected downward, severing an artery. Death had been caused by internal bleeding.

Colebrook's funeral took place in the barracks at Prince Albert on November 2. He was buried in St. Mary's Cemetery in a plot with several police killed in the Riel Rebellion. Mourners included ex-constable Ernest Grundy, now postmaster for the little village of Duck Lake. A close friend of the murdered man, Grundy was to play a tragic role attempting to avenge the death of his friend.

In the following weeks, though rumor spurred frequent patrols through the district, the trail grew cold. Almighty Voice's wife was released in the hope that she might lead the police to him, but she merely returned to John Sounding Sky's cabin on One Arrow's reserve. The only development was that Sergeant Harry Keenan, the NCO in charge of Duck Lake Detachment when Almighty Voice escaped, was demoted to constable.

This demotion caused an immediate public reaction, spearheaded by the vitriolic editor of the *Saskatchewan Times* in Prince Albert. Harry Keenan had been one of the first men to join the North-West Mounted Police when it was formed, enlisting November 3, 1873. He resigned after nine years of service during which time he rose to sergeant, but re-enlisted the following year and quickly reached his former rank. During the unrest which preceded the 1885 Riel uprising, Keenan had effectively scouted the rebels and gave the first warning that they intended to defy the Canadian government. As a result of the public's defense of Keenan, Commissioner Herchmer re-instated him to his former rank.

In the months that followed, Almighty Voice drifted from band to lonely band of Crees. He appeared sometimes at the John Smith Reservation at Fort a la Corne, at other times with the bands near Nut and Quill Lakes where he had many relatives. In April 1896, the Canadian government offered a reward of $500 for information leading to his capture but the offer solved nothing.

In the meantime, police officers suspected that Almighty Voice had not fled far from his familiar surroundings. In the spring of 1897 his wife gave birth to a son, Stanislaus. Then in May, David and Napoleon Venne, sons of a Metis farmer who lived east of One Arrow's reserve, noticed

Officer Colebrook, second from left with rifle, as a Constable in 1885. He is standing behind Big Bear after the rebel chief's capture during the Riel Rebellion.

three Indians chasing their cattle. They pursued the trio to one of the dense poplar bluffs that dotted the rolling prairie.

One of the apparent cattle thieves met misfortune when his pony stumbled in a gopher hole and threw him. Before he could regain his mount he was captured by the Venne brothers. He gave his name as Little Salteau and named one of his escaped companions as Dubling. The Vennes became suspicious. Little Salteau refused to divulge the third man's identity. But as they had nothing definite to act upon they released their prisoner.

The following morning they discovered that one of their cows had been slaughtered during the night. The prime suspects were Little Salteau and his companions. Napoleon Venne rode to the NWMP detachment at Batoche, then under command of Corporal William Bowridge.

Bowridge also thought that the unnamed Indian might well be Almighty Voice and he rode back to the Venne farm to inspect the cow's carcass. The fact that the bulk of the carcass was intact made him more suspicious and he went directly to John Sounding Sky's cabin. While there was no sign of Almighty Voice, Bowridge learned that Dubling had traded a horse for a rifle the night before.

During his search of the reservation land, Corporal Bowridge saw two Indians run into a poplar bluff. He rode towards the bluff with Venne at his side. It proved a dangerous move. As they approached the poplar copse, two rifle shots rang out. The first bullet struck Venne in the shoulder, the second creased his rifle butt.

Corporal Bowridge assisted his companion to safety and both men returned to Batoche. Venne identified the man who shot him as Dubling. The second man was probably Almighty Voice. After alerting his superior officer, Bowridge arrested John Sounding Sky on a charge of being an accessory after the fact to the murder of Sergeant Colebrook in October 1895.

Within an hour after Inspector Allen at Prince Albert received word of the incident he had nine men ready for action. The detail was handed over to Sergeant Charles Raven with orders to proceed to the reservation. Then Inspector Allen left for McDowell to pick up a guide and interpreter.

Early on May 28, the two parties met at the St. Louis de Langevin ferry and set out for the Minichinis Hills east of One Arrow's reserve where Venne had been shot. Leaving before the main party of police were ready, Inspector Allen reconnoitered the surrounding area from a hill overlooking the prairie. He noticed a movement in the valley to the east but was unable to determine whether the objects were men or deer. In the meantime, a messenger arrived from Sergeant Raven advising the men had been sighted east of the Venne farm.

SLAUGHTER AMID THE POPLARS

Meanwhile, Sergeant Raven's men were combing the countryside on both sides of the trail leading to Touchwood Hills. At one point Constable C.M. McNair reported sighting three objects moving ahead of the posse and the search was intensified. A few moments later, Constable Andrew O'Kelly — the man who had first discovered Almighty Voice's absence from the Duck Lake Jail — confirmed he had seen three Indians disappear into a bluff of poplars about 180 m (600 ft.) ahead.

Without waiting for Allen, Raven called in his outriders and rode forward to the bluff. The stand of trees extended in a north-south direction and was heavily overgrown with underbrush. In places it was difficult to see more than a few feet. As he detailed his men to surround the bluff, Raven saw Inspector Allen and guide William Bruce approaching along the main road from the Venne farm.

Taking Constable William Hume, a crack revolver shot, Raven rode to the north end of the bluff and dismounted. He planned to traverse the woods from north to south, and by keeping an equal distance from each edge of the bluff and from each other, cover the entire area in one sweep.

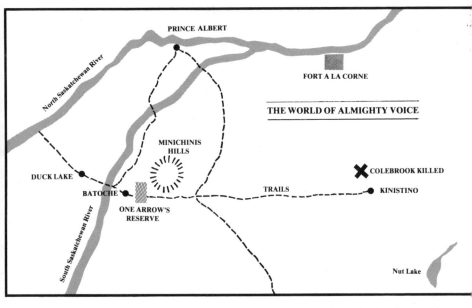

With his carbine, a shell in the breech, Raven started into the bush. To his right Constable Hume advanced abreast, revolver ready.

Sergeant Raven later wrote: "We had gone about 50 yards when I came to a narrow opening in the underbrush and caught a glimpse of two Indians, crouched down, about 20 yards from me. They had rifles and fired at once and disappeared in the brush. I fired in their direction, as did Constable Hume, but without result . . . ."

Again the Indians had demonstrated their skill with their rifles. Raven was hit twice in the hip, his leg numb and useless. He was dragged from the underbrush by his comrade. Despite the wound, Raven shouted a warning to the men encircling the bluff to watch out for the Indians now crashing toward the south end of the copse. Then Raven collapsed.

The constables stationed at intervals round the bluff could see nothing. Although they heard at least five shots, they could only hold their ground and scan the edge of the woods. Inspector Allen, who arrived as Raven was dragged to open ground, demanded: "Who is running? What was that shooting about?"

The wounded Raven weakly answered that he was certain one of the men was Almighty Voice trying to escape from the southern end of the copse.

Drawing his revolver, Allen spurred his horse southward along the edge of the bluff and swung into an opening in the willow scrub. He was suddenly confronted by three Indians intent on gaining the open ground. "Here they are, boys!" Allen shouted.

The same instant, Almighty Voice and his companions fired. A heavy slug shattered Allen's right arm and he thudded to the ground. Almighty Voice jumped from shelter and advanced cautiously. Realizing that he and his companions were trapped, his first thought was to secure the fallen officer's ammunition belt.

Later, Inspector Allen recalled the incident: "Pulling myself through the twigs to a small ash stump, I was enabled to come to my feet, only to find myself looking into the barrel of an old pattern .45-75 Winchester. Almighty Voice . . . had me covered. The other two Indians had jumped back to safety."

Constable McNair who was stationed back from the bluff fired a long shot at the wanted criminal. A few seconds later, Sergeant Raven, realizing Allen's plight, dragged himself upright and opened fire from long range. Constable Hume disregarded his own safety by rushing headlong to the Inspector's assistance, firing rapidly from his service revolver. Almighty Voice ignored the ammunition belt and scrambled into the underbrush.

Corporal C. Hockin and Constable J.R. Kerr heard the fusillade from their posts on the west side of the bluff and spurred their horses to where Allen had been ambushed. They opened fire at the spot where the three Indians had last been seen. Hume had meanwhile reached the unconscious Inspector Allen. Ignoring the desultory sniping from the fugitives, the constable hoisted Allen onto his horse and carried him to safety.

Despite severe wounds, Sergeant Raven returned to the task of resetting his men round the bluff, hoping to prevent the three men from escaping. Then Inspector Allen recovered consciousness and sent Constable O'Kelly to Batoche to alert the rest of the detachments and to bring medical aid. A short time later, Allen was placed onto a wagon and driven towards Prince Albert.

DEADLY CONFLICT

Almighty Voice, Dubling and Little Salteau, surrounded by grim-faced policemen, celebrated their first victory by an impromptu war dance, their hideous screams plainly audible to the men. After a few random shots were pumped into the woods, the war cries ceased. Silence hung over the woods.

At noon a tentative attempt was made to set fire to the woods, but the grass and trees were too green to ignite. In the late afternoon, an impromptu posse comprising Dr. Stewart from the Indian Agency, Constable A. O'Kelly and five civilians arrived from Batoche and Duck Lake. One of the civilians was postmaster Ernest Grundy, the ex-constable and close friend of the slain Sergeant Colebrook. The wounded Sergeant

Raven was immediately taken to Duck Lake in a buckboard and Corporal Hockin took charge.

As evening approached, Corporal Hockin faced a difficult decision. A cloudy sky suggested that the night would be dark, affording ample opportunity for Almighty Voice and his companions to slip through the cordon of police and volunteers. He conferred with Constable Kelly and the civilians and decided to search the bluff rather than risk losing the three Indians in the darkness. All concerned had no illusions about the risks but none could imagine the disaster soon to take place.

To add to the difficulties of those besieging the bluff, Indians from the One Arrow Reserve began to arrive. Keeping a respectful distance, they made camp on a low hill overlooking the scene. Spotted Calf, Almighty Voice's mother, was among them.

Corporal Hocking suspected that Almighty Voice and his friends might have worked their way towards the north end of the bluff where Raven and Hume had first encountered them. As a consequence he stationed the civilians at vantage points but concentrated them along the southern edge. Then at the head of nine men, he walked to the north end of the woods.

Instead of working his way southward, as did Raven and Hume, the Corporal decided to traverse the bluff in an east-west direction. He stationed his men in a line, almost shoulder to shoulder. Forcing through the thick underbrush, the ten men worked their way slowly from one side of the bluff to the other. Without a shot being fired, they emerged on the west side.

They traversed the woods a second time, expecting every moment to be confronted by the crack of rifles. When they emerged on the east side facing the road, they were met by Corporal Bowridge who took his place in the line as they wheeled for the third approach. As Corporal Hockin moved his men closer to the south end of the bluff he felt the tension mount. He knew it was impossible for the Indians to have escaped. They had to be in the woods. He also knew that they were deadly shots.

Hockin gave the command and the line moved slowly forward. Faces were stern and fingers closed tensely over revolver butts. Step by step the line worked through the willow underbrush. It reached the halfway point with no sign of the concealed desperadoes.

Centering the line — Ernest Grundy on one side, Constable Kerr on the other — Hockin pushed forward. They were almost to the west side of the woods when a burst of gunfire crashed out with startling bitterness.

Grundy dropped, shot through the stomach. Corporal Hockin staggered, a bullet in his chest. On either side of the fatally wounded men, posse members flung themselves down to escape a second fusillade. Desperately they searched the impenetrable screen of grass and willow to locate the ambush. All was silent. After their deadly volley, Almighty Voice and his companions patiently awaited their pursuers' next move.

It was Constable Kerr who detected a slight movement in the underbrush. Signalling to O'Kelly, Kerr pointed and indicated that he was going to charge. O'Kelly nodded his readiness. Simultaneously, the two policemen leaped to their feet and ran towards a low pile of logs. They had

Napoleon Venne was among those wounded and fortunate to live.

Almighty Voice's deadly rifle.

Postmaster Ernest Grundy was killed, leaving a wife and four children.

scarcely moved before a volley shattered the silent woods and Kerr slumped forward, a bullet through his heart.

Constable O'Kelly dropped to the ground and worked his way back to the wounded Corporal Hockin. Nearby members of the search party opened fire on the logs but a steady return fire warned them not to expose their position.

The command to retire was given. With painstaking care the remaining men worked their way back through the underbrush — feet first and heads in the direction of the ambush. With assistance, O'Kelly dragged the inert Hockin with him. No attempt was made to rescue Kerr whose body was in full view of the concealed rifle pit. Postmaster Grundy had died and he, too, had to be left.

As the posse emerged from the bluff, Indian Farm Instructor Marion who had been vainly trying to persuade the watching Indians to return to the reserve, leaped into his wagon and raced towards the woods. The wounded corporal was drawn to the safety of the road. Even as he was being placed in the wagon, a long-range shot from the bluff caught a civilian in the heel.

Although Dr. Stewart rendered immediate attention, Hockin's wound proved fatal and he died on the way to the hospital at Duck Lake.

As darkness fell over the Minichinis Hills, the police kept all night vigil by the light of huge bonfires circling the bluff. The incident which began with a wandering cow of no known origin had now claimed four lives. Those watching the bluff couldn't help wondering who would be next.

DEATH SONG

At Prince Albert, telegraphic despatches told of mounting casualties and that the Indians from One Arrow Reserve were moving slowly to the scene of the fighting. Fearing another uprising, Superintendent Severe Gagnon organized members of the Prince Albert Volunteers, a militia group that had seen active service during the Riel Rebellion.

From detailed reports Gagnon realized that the three Indians were in an advantageous position and he resolved to treat the matter as a military campaign. Readying the brass 7-pounder cannon at the detachment, he loaded a wagon with shells and prepared to set off. Then it was discovered that no one in the force knew how to fire the cannon. Further delay ensued while a civilian was commandeered to operate it.

Late in the night with eight police and volunteers — among them Surgeon Bain and Hospital Sergeant West — Gagnon left Prince Albert. On Saturday morning, May 29, the group reached the ferry over the South Saskatchewan River at McKenzie Crossing. Here Gagnon met the wounded Inspector Allen. As Surgeon Bain dressed the policeman's shattered arm, Gagnon learned of the problems confronting the police and civilians at the bluff. After an early breakfast he led the little column southward towards the poplar bluff and its murderous occupants.

Meanwhile, Commissioner Herchmer of Regina had been kept informed by telegraph. On Friday morning he learned of the wounding of Captain Allan and Sergeant Raven and decided to send ten more policemen to the area. That night, however, during a ball in honor of a police

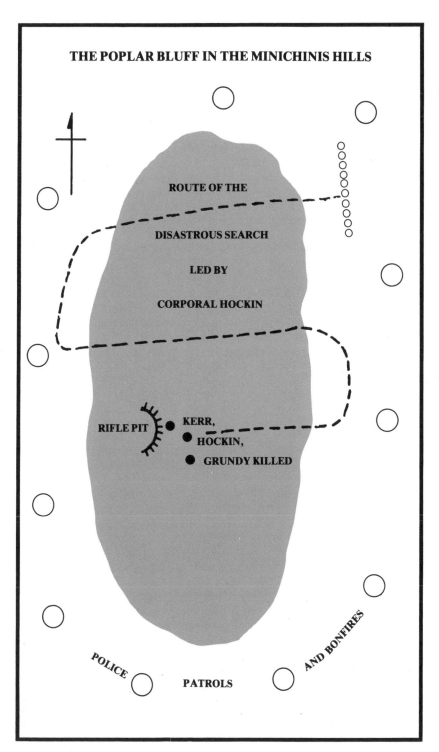

THE POPLAR BLUFF IN THE MINICHINIS HILLS

ROUTE OF THE

DISASTROUS SEARCH

LED BY

CORPORAL HOCKIN

RIFLE PIT

KERR,

HOCKIN,

GRUNDY KILLED

POLICE

PATROLS

AND BONFIRES

contingent leaving to participate in Queen Victoria's Diamond Jubilee Celebrations, Herchmer received more ominous news. As *The Leader* at Regina reported:

". . . Just before midnight, and while a waltz was in progress, Commissioner Herchmer got the message of the killing of Corp. Hockin, Const. Kerr and Mr. Grundy. Suddenly the music ceased and the reason of its cessation passed quickly around. The dance was ended. Upon further information received during the night, the Commissioner decided to send out a larger force than was first intended. The bustle of loading a field piece, and horses, and the sending of so considerable a force as twenty-five men, with the Asst. Commissioner, aroused no little excitement. The regular train being unable to exceed schedule time, a special was chartered. It may be noted that it was just 30 minutes after C.P.R. Agent Birbeck was given the order for a special train, that it left the depot towards the scene of action . . . ."

With the policemen went a correspondent from *The Leader* who wrote the following account:

"The last sound from friends that greeted the Regina detachment of the N.W.M.P. as they left to capture Almighty Voice was the ringing cheer of the citizens as the train drew out of the depot. The men were pleased with this recognition and it made them more determined than ever that, so far as they were concerned, Almighty Voice was doomed — to be either caught or killed. This was at half-past ten on Saturday morning, and by

4:50 p.m. we were at Duck Lake station, after the fastest run ever made on the Prince Albert branch . . . . The force then set off to Batoche, crossed One Arrow's reserve and passed through the Belle Vue settlement to Minetchinase (Minichinis), or 'the beautiful bare hills' amid which Almighty Voice had been driven to bay . . . .

"The ride and drive through the beautiful country was very enjoyable. The scenery is magnificent, with the noble river and the splendid bluffs, rich in Spring's pride so luxuriant that it well might be their summer's glory, and above all the witchery of a soft blue sky on which faintly shone filmy cloud delicately ringed by the setting sun. The great orb had sunk to his rest by the time the gun equipage had reached Batoche ferry . . . .

". . . At Batoche *The Leader* man was informed that Almighty Voice ought to have been hunted down long ago. It has been known for several months past that he was in the neighborhood. Old John, his father, had been seen periodically carrying provisions to him, seldom at more than a week apart. Old John is regarded with as much dread as Almighty Voice. Indeed many persons think it was he who shot Venne, with whom he was at enmity and had vowed to exterminate the whole family. It is indeed likely he did fire at Venne. Certainly he was with Almighty Voice at the time and it seems to have escaped the notice of the reporters that Venne, in addition to the bullet-wound in his shoulder, was peppered with shot in the leg. People were glad, therefore, that Old John had been arrested and it is

A NWMP artillery detachment practice loading their field guns in 1894.

hoped that he will not be liberated: because, it is said, trouble will be certain to follow.

"While driving through the reserve we passed the home of Almighty Voice. His wife was standing on the threshold. She made a motion as we passed: but whether it was intended to express encouragement, derision or contempt it was too dark to see, but from the temper shown all along it was likely a gesture of defiance. It was eleven o'clock at night when the last of the four equipage rigs arrived at the camp. It was very dark and a slight mist hung over the ground. It was a night most favorable for crawling out of a bluff, and this made the sentries all the more determined to keep alert. The men from Prince Albert, Duck Lake and Batoche were at their third night's watch, having had but the roughest of food snatched at intervals, and so little rest that not a kit had been unrolled. The cordon round the bluff was strengthened by the Regina men, and it was felt that the outlaw was so hemmed in that escape was impossible. The mother of Almighty Voice visited the camp. She said: 'There are many of you and you may catch him and kill him, but he will kill many of you first . . . .'

". . . The Indian 'Doubling' (also spelled Dubling) came to the edge of the bluff and shouted something in Cree. What he said is not exactly known. One person translated it as a defiant message thus: 'You have fired long but you will have to do better than that.' Another says that what Doubling said was: 'You have fired long, now send us something to eat,' which, as after events showed, is much more probable.

"The night was a night of watching, cold and dark. A few of us who were not watching stood round a camp fire longing for the dawn and what it would bring forth. The monotony was relieved by an occasional per-ambulation of the pickets and the only sound heard was the frequent click of a carbine as a sentry, or more than one, fired at one or other of the occupants of the bluff. On one occasion sentries fired at opposite ends of the bluff at the same time, and it is pretty certain that the two Indians were simultaneously endeavoring to leave the bluff in opposite directions . . . ."

". . . Once a bullet came whizzing amongst us who were standing round the fire, a visitor that certainly was not particularly welcome. At the first faint streak of dawn there was a lively rattle from the Winchesters all round the bluff, as though in the dim light the whole cordon imagined they saw the enemy.

"The time had now arrived for preparing for the day's work. The horses were taken to the nearest water, a mile away. Ultimately the team was fixed to the nine-pounder and it was drawn to a position covering the corner of the bluff opposite to where the seven-pounder was pointed. Precisely at six o'clock both cannons opened fire. . . . Smith guided the nine-pounder with deadly aim, and Walton did destructive work with the seven-pounder that had distinguished itself at the Duck Lake fight in 1885. For an hour a perfect shower of shrapnel and grape was poured into the bluff. The shells were timed to burst with admirable precision at 700 yards and it is difficult to imagine that any portion of the bluff escaped the deadly missiles. Neither of the Indians gave any sign of their appreciation of these attentions. The nine-pounder was christened 'Almighty Voice . . . .'

Graves of the slain policemen — Colebrook center; Kerr, left center; Hockin, right center. Almighty Voice was buried where he was killed.

"At ten o'clock the firing ceased, and all was silence . . . . *The Leader* representative preached the doctrine that the men were either dead or had escaped, because the habitual wail to the gods had not been heard that morning, and this is a point savages never neglect. Subsequent events showed that his assumption was not far astray. After a short time people showed signs of weariness at waiting, and a rush on the bluff was talked of. Asst.-Com. McIlree, however, did not think the time had arrived for that, consistent with the orders he had received. The orders before leaving Regina were that he was not to rush the bluff until he was satisfied that all had been done with the guns that could be done, as it was useless to risk any lives when it was certain that the outlaws could not escape, and it was cheaper to pay for special trains than to risk lives . . . . The Asst.-Commissioner decided on another plan. He decided to dig out the culprits. Messengers were despatched to Duck Lake and Prince Albert to get shovels, mattocks and grub hoes. With these, trenches or ditches were to be dug so that the attackers, under cover, could get right up to where the men were hiding.

"Before the implements to do this arrived, however, the patience of the Volunteers was exhausted, and they determined to storm the bluff. . . . McIlree was consulted and explained his orders. The men, however, kept to their determination, and there was nothing left for it but for the police to take the lead in the dash. A splendid rush was made, accompanied by a vigorous fusilade. Asst.-Com. McIlree, Insp. Macdonnell, and Insp. Wilson led the police with a gallant dash. Wm. Drain (one of Riel's capturers) Thos. McKay, Timber-Agent Cook and others led on the Volunteers of Prince Albert and Batoche, Jas. McKay, Q.C., cheering them on from his horse as he rode by the side of the bluff. It was a brave rush and loses nothing of its gallant quality from the fact that it was unnecessary. The Indians were all dead and the bodies cold. Dr. Bain said they had been dead several hours. Had they been alive it is improbable from the vantage position they had that they could have been captured without the loss of half a dozen men, if not more. Both Indians, Almighty Voice and his youthful companion, had been shelled to death in the very refuge they had so patiently dug for their security. The Voice's skull had been shattered by a piece of exploded shell. Doubling's body was found at a short distance. He had not immediately died from the result of O'Kelly's shot, as had been supposed; because he was dressed in Kerr's uniform and wore his ring. Perhaps, too, poor and brave Kerr had not died immediately from the shot in his lungs, for a bullet had been put through his head and his skull battered in with his own carbine, portions of hair, blood and brain having clung to the lock. Insp. Macdonnell took charge of the Winchester. Perhaps, however, the mutilation was after death.

"The rest is soon told. The Indians were buried on the spot. The bodies of Kerr and Grundy were respectfully taken to Duck Lake to await burial . . . ."

Thus ended the eye-witness account of the newspaper reporter. A thorough search of the bluff failed to locate the presence of any other Indians. Later, Thomas McKay discovered a trail of blood where

Almighty Voice had dragged himself a hundred yards across the open prairie during the night, only to be turned back by the sentries.

By mid afternoon, the clearing around the deadly little patch of poplar trees was deserted. The sequence of events which began with Almighty Voice killing a cow of unknown ownership had ended. Three outlaws were dead, but so were three policemen and a brave postmaster who left a wife and four children to mourn.

Plaque erected by Saskatchewan's Department of Natural Resources near the poplar grove.

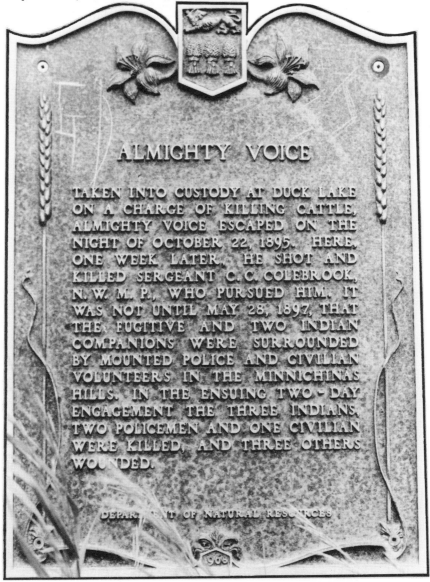

ALMIGHTY VOICE

TAKEN INTO CUSTODY AT DUCK LAKE ON A CHARGE OF KILLING CATTLE, ALMIGHTY VOICE ESCAPED ON THE NIGHT OF OCTOBER 22, 1895. HERE, ONE WEEK LATER, HE SHOT AND KILLED SERGEANT C. C. COLEBROOK, N.W.M.P., WHO PURSUED HIM. IT WAS NOT UNTIL MAY 28, 1897, THAT THE FUGITIVE AND TWO INDIAN COMPANIONS WERE SURROUNDED BY MOUNTED POLICE AND CIVILIAN VOLUNTEERS IN THE MINNICHINAS HILLS. IN THE ENSUING TWO-DAY ENGAGEMENT THE THREE INDIANS, TWO POLICEMEN AND ONE CIVILIAN WERE KILLED, AND THREE OTHERS WOUNDED.

DEPARTMENT OF NATURAL RESOURCES

PROCLAMATION.

ABERDEEN.
(L.S.)

CANADA.

VICTORIA, by the Grace of God, of the United Kingdom of Great Britain and Ireland, *Queen*, Defender of the Faith, &c., &c.

To all to whom these presents shall come, or whom the same may in anywise concern, GREETING:

A PROCLAMATION.

E. L. NEWCOMBE,
Deputy of the Minister of Justice, Canada.

WHEREAS, on the twenty-ninth day of October, one thousand eight hundred and ninety-five, **COLIN CAMPBELL COLEBROOK**, a Sergeant of the North-West Mounted Police, was murdered about eight miles east of Kinistino, or about forty miles south-east of Prince Albert, in the North-West Territories, by an Indian known as "Jean-Baptiste," or "Almighty Voice," who escaped from the police guard-room at Duck Lake;

And Whereas, it is highly important for the peace and safety of Our subjects that such a crime should not remain unpunished, but that the offenders should be apprehended and brought to justice;

Now Know Ye that a reward of **FIVE HUNDRED DOLLARS** will be paid to any person or persons who will give such information as will lead to the apprehension and conviction of the said party.

In Testimony Whereof, We have caused these Our Letters to be made Patent and the Great Seal of Canada to be hereunto affixed. Witness, Our Right Trusty and Right Well-beloved Cousin and Councillor the Right Honourable Sir JOHN CAMPBELL HAMILTON-GORDON, Earl of Aberdeen; Viscount Formartine, Baron Haddo, Methlic, Tarves and Kellie, in the Peerage of Scotland; Viscount Gordon of Aberdeen, County of Aberdeen, in the Peerage of the United Kingdom; Baronet of Nova Scotia, Knight Grand Cross of Our Most Distinguished Order of Saint Michael and Saint George, &c., Governor General of Canada.

At Our Government House, in Our City of Ottawa, this Twentieth day of April, in the year of Our Lord one thousand eight hundred and ninety-six, and in the Fifty-ninth year of Our Reign.

By command,

CHARLES TUPPER,
Secretary of State.

DESCRIPTION OF THE AFORESAID INDIAN "JEAN-BAPTISTE" OR "ALMIGHTY VOICE":

About twenty-two years old, five feet ten inches in height, weight eleven stone, slightly built and erect, neat small feet and hands; complexion inclined to be fair, wavy dark hair to shoulders, large dark eyes, broad forehead, sharp features and parrot nose with flat tip, scar on left cheek running from mouth towards ear, feminine appearance.

The reward notice for the apprehension
of Almighty Voice. (See page 104.)

More Good Reads From Heritage

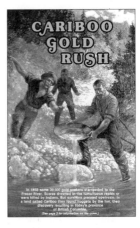

Cariboo Gold Rush

The saga of 30,000 chasing one of the world's richest discoveries in 1858. They found nuggets by the ton and carved a web of trails and memories into the heart of BC. Maps, photos, barroom tales, success, tragedy and characters galore.

0-919214-90-8 • 96 pages • softcover • $7.95

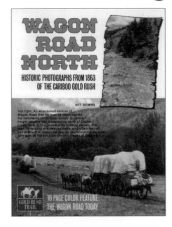

Wagon Road North
Art Downs

One of BC's most popular books with sales over 130,000. Compiled from diaries, journals, eye-witness reports. Over 200 photos including St. Saviour's Church, now over 100 years old, and the nearby 1863 graveyard.

0-9690546-0-2 • 96 pages • softcover • $14.95

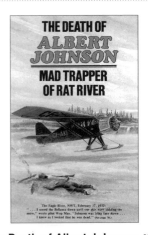

The Death of Albert Johnson Mad Trapper of Rat River

Pursuit of a murderer in the Arctic. It took six weeks and four shoot-outs amid blizzards and numbing cold as a posse of trappers, soldiers, Indians and the RCMP hunted their man. Who was Albert Johnson?

0-919214-16-9 • 96 pages • softcover • $7.95

Cariboo Cowboy
Harry Marriott

Harry started the OK ranch in 1912 and led his last round-up and cattle drive of 1,000 head when he was 70. He recalls cowboys, Indians, homesteaders and fellow ranchers, "Folks who would make you welcome when you rode by."

1-895811-08-2 • 192 pages • softcover • $14.95

Western Canadiana From Heritage

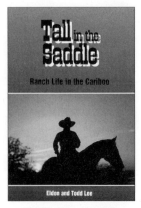

Tall in the Saddle
Eldon and Todd Lee

They had little formal education but a dedicated mother and home learnin' seemed to work. Before they retired Dr. Eldon had delivered 4,000 babies and Reverend Todd had written a host of books. Here they fondly recall their Cariboo ranch days.

1-895811-44-9 • 160 pages • softcover • $14.95

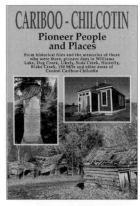

Cariboo-Chilcotin
Irene Stangoe

Drawn from historical files and the memories of those who were there: pioneer days in Williams Lake, Dog Creek, Likely, Soda Creek, Horsefly, Riske Creek, 150 Mile and other areas of Central Cariboo-Chilcotin. Well illustrated with current and historical photos.

1-895811-12-0 • 128 pages • softcover • $11.95

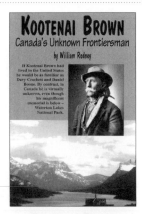

Kootenai Brown
William Rodney

Brown's adventurous life in Canada began in 1862 during the Cariboo gold rush. He was a policeman, a Pony Express Ride who escaped the wrath of Sitting Bull, a Rocky Mountain Ranger and a conservationist.

1-895811-31-7 • 256 pages • softcover • $17.95

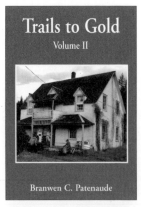

Trails to Gold Volume II
Branwen C. Patenaude

This authoritative work details the history of the roadhouse along the Cariboo Wagon Road, the trail to one of the 19th century's great gold rushes – great anecdotes, many photos., maps and index.

0-895811-09-0 • 224 pages • Softcover • $18.95

Heritage books are available at over 500 locations is Western Canada. If unavailable near you, write #8-17921 55th Avenue, Surrey, BC, V3C 6C4. Include GST and handling cost of $1.00 per order.